DRACULA

Bram Stoker

TECHNICAL DIRECTOR Maxwell Krohn
EDITORIAL DIRECTOR Justin Kestler
MANAGING EDITOR Ben Florman

SERIES EDITORS Boomie Aglietti, Justin Kestler
PRODUCTION Christian Lorentzen, Camille Murphy

WRITERS Ross Douthat, David Hopson
EDITORS Matt Blanchard, Benjamin Morgan

This edition published by Spark Publishing

Spark Publishing
A Division of SparkNotes LLC
120 Fifth Avenue, 8th Floor
New York, NY 10011

Any book purchased without a cover is stolen property, reported as "unsold and destroyed" to the Publisher, who receives no payment for such "stripped books."

02 03 04 05 SN 9 8 7 6 5 4 3 2 1

Please send all comments and questions or report errors to feedback@sparknotes.com.

Library of Congress information available upon request

Printed and bound in the United States

RRD-C

ISBN 1-58663-447-X

Introduction: Stopping to Buy Sparknotes on a Snowy Evening

Whose words these are you *think* you know.
Your paper's due tomorrow, though;
We're glad to see you stopping here
To get some help before you go.

Lost your course? You'll find it here.
Face tests and essays without fear.
Between the words, good grades at stake:
Get great results throughout the year.

Once school bells caused your heart to quake
As teachers circled each mistake.
Use SparkNotes and no longer weep,
Ace every single test you take.

Yes, books are lovely, dark, and deep,
But only what you grasp you keep,
With hours to go before you sleep,
With hours to go before you sleep.

Contents

CONTEXT

BRAM STOKER WAS BORN in Dublin, Ireland, in 1847. The son of a civil servant, Stoker was a sickly child. Stoker's mother, a charity worker and writer, spent a good deal of time entertaining her son with fantastic tales. Stoker went on to study math at Trinity College and graduated in 1867, at which time he joined the Irish civil service. He also worked as a freelance journalist and drama critic, which enabled him to meet the legendary stage actor Henry Irving. The two men became lifelong friends, and Stoker managed Irving's theater from 1878 until Irving's death in 1905. Stoker married an aspiring actress, Florence Balcombe, and the couple had one son, Noel, who was born in 1879. Stoker moved to London in order to oversee Irving's theater, and he fell into the city's literary circles, which included figures such as Oscar Wilde, Arthur Conan Doyle, and Alfred Lord Tennyson.

Stoker's early fiction is not of particularly high quality. He wrote short stories for children and then a first novel, *The Snake's Pass* (1890), which was unsuccessful. Stoker's fortunes changed in 1897 with the publication of *Dracula*, which still stands as his greatest literary achievement. Although the novel was not an immediate popular success, it has been in print continuously since its first publication and has inspired countless films and other literary works. Stoker continued to write until his death in 1912, producing several adventure novels, including *The Jewel of Seven Stars* (1904) and *The Lair of the White Worm* (1911).

Vampire legends have been a part of popular folklore in many parts of the world since ancient times. Throughout the Middle Ages and even into the modern era, reports of corpses rising from the dead with supernatural powers achieved widespread credence. The Dracula family, which Stoker's count describes with pride in the early chapters of the novel, is based on a real fifteenth-century family. Its most famous member, Vlad Dracula—or Vlad the Impaler, as he was commonly known—enjoyed a bloody career that rivaled that of his fictional counterpart. The Prince of Wallachia, Vlad was a brilliant and notoriously savage general who impaled his enemies on long spikes. The prince also had a reputation for murdering beggars, forcing women to eat their babies, and nailing the turbans of disrespectful ambassadors to their heads. While Stoker's Count Dracula is supposed to be a descendant of Vlad, and not the prince himself, Stoker clearly makes the count resemble his fearsome ancestor. This historical allusion gives Dracula a semblance of truth, and, as the Author's Note and the coda make clear, Stoker wants to suggest that the documents assembled in the novel are real.

Stoker also relies heavily on the conventions of Gothic fiction, a genre that was extremely popular in the early nineteenth century. Gothic fiction traditionally includes elements such as gloomy castles, sublime landscapes, and innocent maidens threatened by ineffable evil. Stoker modernizes this tradition in his novel, however, moving from the conventional setting of Dracula's ruined castle into the bustle of modern England. As Stoker portrays the collision of two disparate worlds—the count's ancient Transylvania and the protagonist's modern London—he lays bare many of the anxieties that characterized his age: the repercussions of scientific advancement, the consequences of abandoning traditional beliefs, and the dangers of female sexuality. To this day, *Dracula* remains a fascinating study of popular attitudes toward sex, religion, and science at the end of the nineteenth century.

PLOT OVERVIEW

J ONATHAN HARKER, A YOUNG ENGLISH LAWYER, travels to Castle Dracula in the Eastern European country of Transylvania to conclude a real estate transaction with a nobleman named Count Dracula. As Harker wends his way through the picturesque countryside, the local peasants warn him about his destination, giving him crucifixes and other charms against evil and uttering strange words that Harker later translates into "vampire."

Frightened but no less determined, Harker meets the count's carriage as planned. The journey to the castle is harrowing, and the carriage is nearly attacked by angry wolves along the way. Upon arriving at the crumbling old castle, Harker finds that the elderly Dracula is a well educated and hospitable gentleman. After only a few days, however, Harker realizes that he is effectively a prisoner in the castle.

The more Harker investigates the nature of his confinement, the more uneasy he becomes. He realizes that the count possesses supernatural powers and diabolical ambitions. One evening, Harker is nearly attacked by three beautiful and seductive female vampires, but the count staves them off, telling the vampires that Harker belongs to him. Fearing for his life, Harker attempts to escape from the castle by climbing down the walls.

Meanwhile, in England, Harker's fiancée, Mina Murray, corresponds with her friend Lucy Westenra. Lucy has received marriage proposals from three men—Dr. John Seward, Arthur Holmwood, and an American named Quincey Morris. Though saddened by the fact that she must reject two of these suitors, Lucy accepts Holmwood's proposal.

Mina visits Lucy at the seaside town of Whitby. A Russian ship is wrecked on the shore near the town with all its crew missing and its captain dead. The only sign of life aboard is a large dog that bounds ashore and disappears into the countryside; the only cargo is a set of fifty boxes of earth shipped from Castle Dracula. Not long after, Lucy suddenly begins sleepwalking. One night, Mina finds Lucy in the town cemetery and believes she sees a dark form with glowing red eyes bending over Lucy. Lucy becomes pale and ill, and she bears two tiny red marks at her throat, for which neither Dr. Seward nor Mina can account. Unable to arrive at a satisfactory diagnosis, Dr. Seward sends for his old mentor, Professor Van Helsing.

Suffering from brain fever, Harker reappears in the city of Buda-Pest. Mina goes to join him. Van Helsing arrives in Whitby, and, after his initial examination of Lucy, orders that her chambers be covered with garlic—a traditional charm against vampires. For a time, this effort seems to stave off Lucy's illness. She begins to recover, but her mother, unaware of the garlic's power, unwittingly removes the odiferous plants from the room, leaving Lucy vulnerable to further attack.

Seward and Van Helsing spend several days trying to revive Lucy, performing four blood transfusions. Their efforts ultimately come to nothing. One night, the men momentarily let down their guard, and a wolf breaks into the Westenra house. The shock gives Lucy's mother a fatal heart attack, and the wolf attacks Lucy, killing her.

After Lucy's death, Van Helsing leads Holmwood, Seward, and Quincey Morris to her tomb. Van Helsing convinces the other men that Lucy belongs to the "Un-Dead"—in other words, she has been transformed into a vampire like Dracula. The men remain unconvinced until they see Lucy preying on a defenseless child, which convinces them that she must be destroyed. They agree to follow the ritual of vampire slaying to ensure that Lucy's soul will return to eternal rest. While the undead Lucy sleeps, Holmwood plunges a stake through her heart. The men then cut off her head and stuff her mouth with garlic. After this deed is done, they pledge to destroy Dracula himself.

Now married, Mina and Jonathan return to England and join forces with the others. Mina helps Van Helsing collect the various diary and journal entries that Harker, Seward, and the others have written, attempting to piece together a narrative that will lead them to the count. Learning all they can of Dracula's affairs, Van Helsing and his band track down the boxes of earth that the count uses as a sanctuary during the night from Dracula's castle. Their efforts seem to be going well, but then one of Dr. Seward's mental patients, Renfield, lets Dracula into the asylum where the others are staying, allowing the count to prey upon Mina.

As Mina begins the slow change into a vampire, the men sterilize the boxes of earth, forcing Dracula to flee to the safety of his native Transylvania. The men pursue the count, dividing their forces and tracking him across land and sea. Van Helsing takes Mina with him, and they cleanse Castle Dracula by killing the three female vampires and sealing the entrances with sacred objects. The others catch up with the count just as he is about to reach his castle, and Jonathan and Quincey use knives to destroy him.

Character List

Count Dracula A centuries-old vampire and Transylvanian nobleman, Count Dracula inhabits a crumbling castle in the Carpathian Mountains. Beneath a veneer of aristocratic charm, the count possesses a dark and evil soul. He can assume the form of an animal, control the weather, and he is stronger than twenty men. His powers are limited, however—for instance, he cannot enter a victim's home unless invited, cannot cross water unless carried, and is rendered powerless by daylight.

Van Helsing A Dutch professor, described by his former pupil Dr. Seward as "a philosopher and metaphysician, and one of the most advanced scientists of his day." Called upon to cure the ailing Lucy Westenra, Van Helsing's contributions are essential in the fight against Dracula. Unlike his comrades, Van Helsing is not blinded by the limitations of Western medicine: he knows that he faces a force that cannot be treated with traditional science and reason. Knowledgeable about vampire folklore, Van Helsing becomes Dracula's chief antagonist and the leader of the group that hunts Dracula down and destroys him.

Jonathan Harker A solicitor, or lawyer, whose firm sends him to Transylvania to conclude a real estate transaction with Dracula. Young and naïve, Harker quickly finds himself a prisoner in the castle and barely escapes with his life. He demonstrates a fierce curiosity to discover the true nature of his captor and a strong will to escape. Later, after becoming convinced that the count has moved to London, Harker emerges as a brave and fearless fighter.

Mina Murray Jonathan Harker's fiancée. Mina is a practical young woman who works as a schoolmistress. Eventually victimized by Dracula herself, Mina is also the best friend of the count's first victim in the novel,

Lucy Westenra. Mina is in many ways the heroine of the novel, embodying purity, innocence, and Christian faith—virtues she maintains despite her suffering at the vampire's hands. She is intelligent and resourceful, and her research leads Van Helsing's men to Castle Dracula.

Lucy Westenra Mina's best friend and an attractive, vivacious young woman. The first character in the novel to fall under Dracula's spell, Lucy becomes a vampire, which compromises her much-praised chastity and virtue, and banishes her soul from the promise of eternal rest. Determined that such an end is unfit for an English lady of Lucy's caliber, Van Helsing's crew hunts down the demon she has become and kills it, following the rituals of vampire slaying, and thus restoring Lucy's soul to her body and to heaven.

John Seward A talented young doctor, formerly Van Helsing's pupil. Seward is the administrator of an insane asylum not far from Dracula's English home. Throughout the novel, Seward conducts ambitious interviews with one of his patients, Renfield, in order to understand better the nature of life-consuming psychosis. Although Lucy turns down Seward's marriage proposal, his love for her remains, and he dedicates himself to her care when she suddenly takes ill. After her death, he remains dedicated to fighting the count.

Arthur Holmwood Lucy's fiancé and a friend of her other suitors. Arthur is the son of Lord Godalming and inherits that title upon his father's death. In the course of his fight against Dracula's dark powers, Arthur does whatever circumstances demand: he is the first to offer Lucy a blood transfusion, and he agrees to kill her demonic form.

Quincey Morris A plainspoken American from Texas, and another of Lucy's suitors. Quincey proves himself a brave and good-hearted man, never begrudging Holmwood his success in winning Lucy's hand. Quincey ultimately sacrifices his life in order to rid the world of Dracula's influence.

Renfield A patient at Seward's mental asylum. Variously a strong behemoth and a refined gentleman, Renfield indulges a habit of consuming living creatures—flies, spiders, birds, and so on—which he believes provide him with strength, vitality, and life force.

Mrs. Westenra Lucy's mother. A brittle woman of failing health, Mrs. Westenra inadvertently sabotages her daughter's safety by interfering with Van Helsing's folk remedies. She dies of shock when a wolf leaps through Lucy's bedroom window.

CHARACTER LIST

ANALYSIS OF MAJOR CHARACTERS

COUNT DRACULA

Late in the novel, when Dracula escapes from Van Helsing and company at his Piccadilly house, the count declares, "My revenge is just begun!" It is not immediately clear for what offense Dracula must obtain revenge, but the most convincing answer comes in the opening chapters, when Dracula relates the proud but disappointing history of his family. In Chapter III, he speaks of the "brave races who fought as the lion fights, for lordship." The count notes the power his people once held, but laments the fact that the "warlike days are over."

Although he retains his lordship in Transylvania, the world around him has changed and grown significantly—the "glories" of days gone by now belong to other families and other races. Indeed, when the count discusses "the crowded streets of your mighty London," we sense that he lusts for power and conquest: "I long . . . to be in the midst of the whirl and rush of humanity, to share its life, its change, its death, and all that makes it what it is. But alas!" In this light, Dracula becomes not simply a creature of fathomless evil. Rather, he is a somewhat sympathetic and more human creation, determined to regain his family's lost power and subject the world to his own dark, brutal vision.

VAN HELSING

Old Professor Van Helsing is an experienced, competent man, but due to the unfortunately unskilled manner in which Stoker renders Van Helsing's speech, he often comes across as somewhat bumbling. Nevertheless, Van Helsing emerges as a well-matched adversary to the count, and he is initially the only character who possesses a mind open enough to contemplate and address Dracula's particular brand of evil.

A doctor, philosopher, and metaphysician, Van Helsing arrives on the scene versed not only in the modern methods of Western medicine, but with an unparalleled knowledge of superstitions and folk remedies. He straddles two distinct worlds, the old and the new: the first marked by fearful respect for tradition, the second by ever-progressing modernity. Unlike his former pupil, Dr. Seward, whose obsession with modern techniques blinds him to the real nature of Lucy's sickness, Van Helsing not only diagnoses the young girl's affliction correctly, but offers her the only opportunity for a cure.

Like many of the other characters, Van Helsing is relatively static, as he undergoes no great change or development throughout the course of the novel. Having helped rid the Earth of the count's evil, he departs as he arrived: morally righteous and religiously committed. Van Helsing views his pursuit of Dracula with an air of grandiosity. He envisions his band as "ministers of God's own wish," and assures his comrades that "we go out as the old knights of the Cross to redeem more." Hyperbole aside, Stoker portrays Van Helsing as the embodiment of unswerving good, the hero he recruits "to set the world free."

MINA MURRAY

Mina Murray is the ultimate Victorian woman. Van Helsing's praise of Mina testifies to the fact that she is indeed the embodiment of the virtues of the age. She is "one of God's women, fashioned by His own hand to show us men and other women that there is a heaven where we can enter, and that its light can be here on earth. So true, so sweet, so noble. . . ." Mina stands as the model of domestic propriety, an assistant schoolmistress who dutifully studies newfangled machines like the typewriter so as to be useful to her husband. Unlike Lucy, she is not most noteworthy for her physical beauty, which spares Mina her friend's fate of being transformed into a voluptuous she-devil.

Mina's sexuality remains enigmatic throughout the whole of Dracula. Though she marries, she never gives voice to anything resembling a sexual desire or impulse, which enables her to retain her purity. Indeed, the entire second half of the novel concerns the issue of Mina's purity. Stoker creates suspense about whether Mina, like Lucy, will be lost. Given that Dracula means to use women to access the men of England, Mina's loss could have terrifying repercussions.

We might expect that Mina, who sympathizes with the boldly progressive "New Women" of England, would be doomed to suffer

Lucy's fate as punishment for her progressiveness. But Stoker instead fashions Mina into a goddess of conservative male fantasy. Though resourceful and intelligent enough to conduct the research that leads Van Helsing's crew to the count, Mina is far from a "New Woman" herself. Rather, she is a dutiful wife and mother, and her successes are always in the service of men. Mina's moral perfection remains as stainless, in the end, as her forehead.

LUCY WESTENRA

In many ways, Lucy is much like her dear friend Mina. She is a paragon of virtue and innocence, qualities that draw not one but three suitors to her. Lucy differs from her friend in one crucial aspect, however—she is sexualized. Lucy's physical beauty captivates each of her suitors, and she displays a comfort or playfulness about her desirability that Mina never feels. In an early letter to Mina, Lucy laments, "Why can't they let a girl marry three men, or as many as want her, and save all this trouble?"

Although she chastises herself for this "heresy," her statement indicates that she has desires that cannot be met. Stoker amplifies this faint whisper of Lucy's insatiability to a monstrous volume when he describes the undead Lucy as a wanton creature of ravenous sexual appetite. In this demonic state, Lucy stands as a dangerous threat to men and their tenuous self-control, and therefore, she must be destroyed. Lucy's death returns her to a more harmless state, fixing a look of purity on her face that assures men that the world and its women are exactly as they should be.

THEMES, MOTIFS & SYMBOLS

THEMES

Themes are the fundamental and often universal ideas explored in a literary work.

THE CONSEQUENCES OF MODERNITY

Early in the novel, as Harker becomes uncomfortable with his lodgings and his host at Castle Dracula, he notes that "unless my senses deceive me, the old centuries had, and have, powers of their own which mere 'modernity' cannot kill." Here, Harker voices one of the central concerns of the Victorian era. The end of the nineteenth century brought drastic developments that forced English society to question the systems of belief that had governed it for centuries. Darwin's theory of evolution, for instance, called the validity of long-held sacred religious doctrines into question. Likewise, the Industrial Revolution brought profound economic and social change to the previously agrarian England.

Though Stoker begins his novel in a ruined castle—a traditional Gothic setting—he soon moves the action to Victorian London, where the advancements of modernity are largely responsible for the ease with which the count preys upon English society. When Lucy falls victim to Dracula's spell, neither Mina nor Dr. Seward—both devotees of modern advancements—are equipped even to guess at the cause of Lucy's predicament. Only Van Helsing, whose facility with modern medical techniques is tempered with openmindedness about ancient legends and non-Western folk remedies, comes close to understanding Lucy's affliction.

In Chapter XVII, when Van Helsing warns Seward that "to rid the earth of this terrible monster we must have all the knowledge and all the help which we can get," he literally means *all* the knowledge. Van Helsing works not only to understand modern Western methods, but to incorporate the ancient and foreign schools of thought that the modern West dismisses. "It is the fault of our science," he says, "that it wants to explain all; and if it explain not, then it says there is nothing to explain." Here, Van Helsing points to the dire consequences of subscribing only to contemporary currents of thought. Without an understanding of history—indeed, without different understandings of history—the world is left terribly vulnerable when history inevitably repeats itself.

THE THREAT OF FEMALE SEXUAL EXPRESSION

Most critics agree that Dracula is, as much as anything else, a novel that indulges the Victorian male imagination, particularly regarding the topic of female sexuality. In Victorian England, women's sexual behavior was dictated by society's extremely rigid expectations. A Victorian woman effectively had only two options: she was either a virgin—a model of purity and innocence—or else she was a wife and mother. If she was neither of these, she was considered a whore, and thus of no consequence to society.

By the time Dracula lands in England and begins to work his evil magic on Lucy Westenra, we understand that the impending battle between good and evil will hinge upon female sexuality. Both Lucy and Mina are less like real people than two-dimensional embodiments of virtues that have, over the ages, been coded as female. Both women are chaste, pure, innocent of the world's evils, and devoted to their men. But Dracula threatens to turn the two women into their opposites, into women noted for their voluptuousness—a word Stoker turns to again and again—and unapologetically open sexual desire.

Dracula succeeds in transforming Lucy, and once she becomes a raving vampire vixen, Van Helsing's men see no other option than to destroy her, in order to return her to a purer, more socially respectable state. After Lucy's transformation, the men keep a careful eye on Mina, worried they will lose yet another model of Victorian womanhood to the dark side. The men are so intensely invested in the women's sexual behavior because they are afraid of associating with the socially scorned. In fact, the men fear for nothing less than their own safety. Late in the novel, Dracula mocks Van Helsing's crew, saying, "Your girls that you all love are mine already; and through them you and others shall yet be mine." Here, the count voices a male fantasy that has existed since Adam and Eve were turned out of Eden: namely, that women's ungovernable desires leave men poised for a costly fall from grace.

THE PROMISE OF CHRISTIAN SALVATION

The folk legends and traditions Van Helsing draws upon suggest that the most effective weapons in combating supernatural evil are symbols of unearthly good. Indeed, in the fight against Dracula, these symbols of good take the form of the icons of Christian faith, such as the crucifix. The novel is so invested in the strength and power of these Christian symbols that it reads, at times, like a propagandistic Christian promise of salvation.

Dracula, practically as old as religion itself, stands as a satanic figure, most obviously in his appearance—pointed ears, fangs, and flaming eyes—but also in his consumption of blood. Dracula's bloodthirstiness is a perversion of Christian ritual, as it extends his physical life but cuts him off from any form of spiritual existence. Those who fall under the count's spell, including Lucy Westenra and the three "weird sisters," find themselves cursed with physical life that is eternal but soulless. Stoker takes pains to emphasize the consequences of these women's destruction.

Though they have preyed on helpless children and have sought to bring others into their awful brood, each of the women meets a death that conforms to the Christian promise of salvation. The undead Lucy, for instance, is transformed by her second death into a vision of "unequalled sweetness and purity," and her soul is returned to her, as is a "holy calm" that "was to reign for ever." Even the face of Dracula himself assumes "a look of peace, such as [Mina] never could have imagined might have rested there." Stoker presents a particularly liberal vision of salvation in his implication that the saved need not necessarily be believers. In Dracula, all of the dead are granted the unparalleled peace of salvation—only the "Un-Dead" are barred from it.

MOTIFS

Motifs are recurring structures, contrasts, or literary devices that can help to develop and inform the text's major themes.

BLOOD

Blood functions in many ways in the novel. Its first mention, in Chapter III, comes when the count tells Harker that "blood is too precious a thing in these days of dishonorable peace; and the glories of the great races are as a tale that is told." The count proudly recounts his family history, relating blood to one's ancestry—to the "great races" that have, in Dracula's view, withered. The count fore-tells the coming of a war between lineages: between the East and the West, the ancient and the modern, and the evil and the good.

Later, the depictions of Dracula and his minions feeding on blood suggest the exchange of bodily fluids associated with sexual intercourse: Lucy is "drained" to the point of nearly passing out after the count penetrates her. The vampires' drinking of blood ech-oes the Christian rite of Communion, but in a perverted sense. Rather than gain eternal spiritual life by consuming wine that has been blessed to symbolize Christ's blood, Dracula drinks actual human blood in order to extend his physical—but quite soulless—life. The importance of blood in Christian mythology elevates the battle between Van Helsing's warriors and the count to the signifi-cance of a holy war or crusade.

SCIENCE AND SUPERSTITION

We notice the stamp of modernity almost immediately when the focus of the novel shifts to England. Dr. Seward records his diary on a phonograph, Mina Murray practices typewriting on a newfan-gled machine, and so on. Indeed, the whole of England seems will-ing to walk into a future of progress and advancement. While the peasants of Transylvania busily bless one another against the evil eye at their roadside shrines, Mr. Swales, the poor Englishman whom Lucy and Mina meet in the Whitby cemetery, has no patience for such unfounded superstitions as ghosts and monsters. The threat Dracula poses to London hinges, in large part, on the advance of modernity. Advances in science have caused the English to dismiss the reality of the very superstitions, such as Dracula, that seek to undo their society. Van Helsing bridges this divide: equipped with the unique knowledge of both the East and the West, he represents the best hope of understanding the incomprehensible and ridding the world of evil.

CHRISTIAN ICONOGRAPHY

The icons of Christian, and particularly Catholic, worship appear throughout the novel with great frequency. In the early chapters, the peasants of Eastern Europe offer Jonathan Harker crucifixes to steel him against the malevolence that awaits him. Later, Van Helsing arrives armed with crosses and Communion wafers. The frequency with which Stoker returns to these images frames Van Helsing's mis-sion as an explicitly religious one. He is, as he says near the end of the novel, nothing less than a "minister of God's own wish."

MOTIFS

Symbols

Symbols are objects, characters, figures, or colors used to represent abstract ideas or concepts.

The Weird Sisters

The three beautiful vampires Harker encounters in Dracula's castle are both his dream and his nightmare—indeed, they embody both the dream and the nightmare of the Victorian male imagination in general. The sisters represent what the Victorian ideal stipulates women should not be—voluptuous and sexually aggressive—thus making their beauty both a promise of sexual fulfillment and a curse. These women offer Harker more sexual gratification in two paragraphs than his fiancée Mina does during the course of the entire novel. However, this sexual proficiency threatens to undermine the foundations of a male-dominated society by compromising men's ability to reason and maintain control. For this reason, the sexually aggressive women in the novel must be destroyed.

The Stake Driven Through Lucy's Heart

Arthur Holmwood buries a stake deep in Lucy's heart in order to kill the demon she has become and to return her to the state of purity and innocence he so values. The language with which Stoker describes this violent act is unmistakably sexual, and the stake is an unambiguous symbol for the penis. In this way, it is fitting that the blow comes from Lucy's fiancé, Arthur Holmwood: Lucy is being punished not only for being a vampire, but also for being available to the vampire's seduction—Dracula, we recall, only has the power to attack willing victims. When Holmwood slays the demonic Lucy, he returns her to the role of a legitimate, monogamous lover, which reinvests his fiancée with her initial Victorian virtue.

The Czarina Catherine

The Czarina Catherine is the name of the ship in which Dracula flees England and journeys back to his homeland. The name of ship is taken from the Russian empress who was notorious for her promiscuity. This reference is particularly suggestive of the threat that hangs over Mina Harker's head: should Van Helsing and his men fail, she will be transformed into the same creature of appetites as Lucy.

Summary & Analysis

Chapter I

Summary

Dracula begins with the diary kept by Jonathan Harker—an English solicitor, or lawyer—as he makes his way from England to Eastern Europe. Embarking on his first professional assignment as a solicitor, Harker is traveling to the castle of Count Dracula, a Transylvanian nobleman. Harker hopes to conclude a real estate deal to sell Count Dracula a residence in London. Harker plans to take copious notes throughout his journey so that he can share the details of his adventures with his fiancée, Mina Murray.

In his first diary entry, on May 3, Harker describes the picturesque countryside of Eastern Europe and the exotic food he has tasted at the roadside inns. He notes several recipes that he plans to obtain for Mina. Harker arrives in the northern Romanian town of Bistritz and checks into a hotel Count Dracula has recommended to him. The innkeeper gives Harker a letter from the count. The letter welcomes Harker to the beautiful Carpathian Mountains and informs him that he should take the next day's coach to the Borgo Pass, where a carriage will meet him to bring him the rest of the way to the castle.

As Harker prepares to leave the next morning, the innkeeper's wife delivers an ominous warning. She reminds Harker that it is the eve of St. George's Day, when "all the evil things in the world will have full sway." She then puts a crucifix around his neck. Though he is a practicing Anglican who regards Catholic paraphernalia as somewhat idolatrous, Harker politely accepts the crucifix. He is somewhat disturbed by this exchange, however, and his uneasiness increases when a crowd of peasants gathers around the inn as he boards the coach. They mutter many "queer words" at Harker, which, with the help of his dictionary, he translates to mean "werewolf" or "vampire." As the coach departs, everyone in the crowd makes the sign of the cross in his direction, a gesture that a fellow passenger explains is meant to protect him from the "evil eye."

The journey to the Borgo Pass takes Harker through incomparably beautiful country. At dusk, he passes by quaintly attired peasants kneeling in prayer at roadside shrines. As darkness falls, the other passengers become restless, urging the coachmen to quicken their speed. The driver whips the horses into a frenzy and the coach rockets along the mountain road. One by one, the passengers begin to offer Harker small gifts and tokens that he assumes are also meant to ward off the evil eye.

The coach soon arrives at the Borgo Pass, but there is no carriage waiting to ferry Harker to his final destination. Just as the driver offers to bring Harker back to the pass the next day, however, a small, horse-drawn carriage arrives. Harker boards the carriage and continues toward the castle. He has the impression that the carriage is covering the same ground over and over again, and he grows increasingly fearful as the ride progresses. Harker is spooked several times by the wild howling of wolves.

At one point, Harker looks outside the carriage and sees a flickering blue flame burning somewhere in the distance. The driver pulls over without explanation, inspects the flame, then returns to the carriage and continues on. Harker recounts several more stops to inspect similar flames and notes that at one point, when the driver gathers a few stones around one of the flames, he seems to be able to see the flame through the driver's body. Eventually, Harker arrives, paralyzed by fear, at the dark and ruined castle.

ANALYSIS

Though Stoker wrote *Dracula* well after the heyday of the Gothic novel—the period from approximately 1760 to 1820—the novel draws on many conventions of the genre, especially in these opening chapters. Conceived primarily as bloodcurdling tales of horror, Gothic novels tend to feature strong supernatural elements juxtaposed with familiar backdrops: dark and stormy nights, ruined castles riddled with secret passages, and forces of unlikely good pitted against those of unimaginable evil. Stoker echoes these conventions in this chapter, as the frantic superstitions of the Carpathian peasants, the cold and desolate mountain pass, and Harker's disorienting and threatening ride to Dracula's castle combine to create a mood of doom and dread.

As contemporary readers, we may find the setting vaguely reminiscent of Halloween, but Stoker's descriptions in fact reveal a great deal about nineteenth-century British stereotypes of Eastern Europe. As Harker approaches Dracula's castle, he notes that his trip has been "so strange and uncanny that a dreadful fear came upon [him]." Harker's sense of dread illustrates his inability to comprehend the superstitions of the Carpathian peasants.

Indeed, as an Englishman who "visits the British Museum" in an attempt to understand the lands and customs of Transylvania, Harker emerges as a model of Victorian reason, a clear product of turn-of-the-century England. Harker's education, as well as his Western sense of progress and propriety, disables him from making sense of such rustic traditions as "the evil eye." To a man of Harker's position and education, the strange sights he witnesses en route to the castle strike him as rare curiosities or dreams. He already begins doubting the reality of his experience: "I think I must have fallen asleep and kept dreaming. . . ." Harker's inability to accept what is unknown, irrational, and unprovable is echoed by his English and American compatriots later in the novel. Harker's experience suggests that the foundations of Western civilization—reason, scientific advancement, and economic domination—are threatened by the alternative knowledge that they presume to have surpassed. Western empirical knowledge is vulnerable because it has summarily dismissed foreign ways of thinking and, in doing so, has failed to recognize the power of such alternative modes of thought.

Harker's description of his ascent to the castle as "uncanny" foreshadows the psychological horror of the novel. In 1919, Sigmund Freud published an essay called "The Uncanny," in which he analyzed the implications of feelings and sensations that arouse "dread and horror." Freud concludes that uncanny experiences can arise at two times. First, they can arise when primitive, supposedly disproved beliefs suddenly seem to be confirmed or validated once again. Second, the uncanny can arise when repressed infantile complexes are revived. Most academic criticism of *Dracula* relies heavily on such psychoanalytic theory and argues that the novel can be seen as a case study of repressed instincts coming to the surface. Indeed, such a reading seems inevitable if one considers Freud's model of psychosexual development, which links the first stage of this development—the oral stage—with the death instinct, the urge to destroy what is living. The vampire, bringing about death with his mouth, serves as a fitting embodiment of these abstract psychological concepts, and allows Stoker to investigate Victorian sexuality and repression.

CHAPTERS II–IV

SUMMARY: CHAPTER II

Jonathan Harker stands outside Dracula's remarkable castle, wondering what sort of adventure he has gotten himself into. After a long wait, the count appears and welcomes Harker. Clad in black, he is a tall old man, who is clean-shaven aside from a long, white moustache. When the two shake hands, Harker is impressed by the strength of Dracula's grip, but notes that the ice-cold hand is more like that of a dead man than a living one. Still, the count's greeting is so warm that the Englishman's fears vanish. Harker enters and takes his dinner before a roaring fire. As the two converse, Harker notices what calls Dracula's "marked physiognomy": the count has pointed ears, exceptionally pale skin, and extremely sharp teeth. Harker's nervousness and fears return.

The next day, Harker wakes to find a note from Dracula, excusing himself for the day. Left to himself, Harker enjoys a hearty meal and, encountering no servants in the castle, explores his bedroom and the unlocked room adjacent to it. He sees expensive furniture, rich tapestries and fabrics, and a library filled with reading material in English—but notes that there are no mirrors to be found anywhere.

That evening, Dracula joins Harker for conversation in the library, as he is eager to learn inflections of English speech before moving to his new estate. The men discuss the pervasiveness of evil spirits in Transylvania. Harker describes the house that the count has purchased: it is an old mansion called Carfax, quite isolated, with only a lunatic asylum and an old chapel nearby. Dracula draws out the conversation long into the night, but abruptly leaves his guest at daybreak. The count's strange behavior increases Harker's sense of uneasiness.

The next day, Dracula interrupts Harker shaving. Harker is startled and accidentally cuts himself. Glancing at his shaving mirror, he notices that the count has no reflection. Harker is also startled by Dracula's reaction to the sight of his blood: the count lunges for his guest's throat, drawing back only after touching the string of beads that holds Harker's crucifix. After warning Harker against cutting himself in this country, Dracula throws the shaving mirror out a window. Left alone, Harker eats breakfast, noting that he has never seen his host eat or drink. His suspicions aroused, he once again goes exploring, only to discover one locked door after another. Harker realizes he is a prisoner in the count's castle.

SUMMARY: CHAPTER III

That night, Harker questions his host about the history of Transylvania. Dracula speaks enthusiastically of the country's people and battles, and he boasts of the glories of his family name. Over the course of the next several days, the count, in turn, grills Harker about matters of English life and law. He tells Harker to write letters to his fiancée and employer, telling them that he will extend his stay in Transylvania by a month. Feeling obliged to his firm and overpowered by the count, Harker agrees. Preparing to take his leave for the evening, Dracula warns his guest never to fall asleep anywhere in the castle other than his own room. Harker hangs his crucifix above his bed and, satisfied that the count has departed, sets out to explore the castle. Peering out a window, Harker observes Dracula crawling down the sheer face of the castle. He wonders what kind of creature the count is and fears that there will be no escape.

One evening soon thereafter, Harker forces a locked room open and falls asleep, not heeding the count's warning. Harker is visited—whether in a dream or not, he cannot say—by three beautiful women with inhumanly red lips and sharp teeth. The women approach him, filling him with a "wicked, burning desire." Just as one of the voluptuous women bends and places her lips against his neck, Dracula sweeps in, ordering the women to leave Harker alone. "When I am done with him you shall kiss him at your will," the count tells them. To appease the disappointed trio, Dracula offers them a bag containing a small, "half-smothered" child. The terrible women seem to fade out of the room as Harker drifts into unconsciousness.

SUMMARY: CHAPTER IV

Harker wakes up in his own bed, unsure whether the previous night's experience was a dream or reality. Several days later, Dracula asks Harker write three letters to his fiancée and employer, and to date them June 12, 19, and 29, even though it is currently only May 19. The count instructs Harker to write that he has left the castle and is safely on his way home.

Meanwhile, a party of Gypsies has come to the castle, and Harker, hoping for a chance to escape, resolves to ask them to send a letter to Mina. Harker passes his secret correspondence to a Gypsy through the bars of his window. Later that evening, Dracula appears with the letter in hand, declaring that it is a vile outrage upon his friendship and hospitality, and burns it.

Weeks pass. It is now mid-June, and Harker remains a prisoner. More Gypsies arrive at the castle, and Harker sees them unloading large wooden boxes from a wagon. One day, having discovered that several articles of his clothing have disappeared for some "new scheme of villainy," Harker witnesses the count slithering down the castle wall wearing Harker's suit. Dracula carries a bundle much like the one earlier devoured by the three terrible women, which convinces Harker that his host is using the disguise to commit unspeakable deeds.

Later that day, a distraught woman appears at the castle gate, wailing for her child. A pack of wolves emerges from the courtyard and devours her. Desperate, Harker resolves to scale a portion of the castle wall in order to reach Dracula's room during the day. He manages the feat and finds the count's room empty except for a heap of gold. Discovering a dark, winding stairway, Harker follows it and encounters fifty boxes of earth in a tunnel-like passage. Harker opens several of the boxes and discovers the count in one of them, either dead or asleep. Terrified, Harker flees back to his room.

On June 29, Dracula promises Harker that he can leave the next day, but Harker requests to leave immediately. Though his host agrees and opens the front door, Harker's departure is impeded by a waiting pack of wolves. Later, overhearing the count say, "To-night is mine. To-morrow night is yours!" Harker opens his bedroom door to find the three voluptuous women. He returns to his room and prays for his safety.

In the morning, Harker wakes early and climbs down to the count's room again. Dracula is asleep as before, but looks younger and sleeker, and Harker notices blood trickling down from the corners of his mouth. Harker takes up a shovel, meaning to kill the vampire, but the blow glances harmlessly off the count's forehead. Harker resolves to take some of Dracula's gold and attempt to escape by descending the castle wall. His entry ends with a desperate, "Good-bye, all! Mina!"

────────────────

ANALYSIS: CHAPTERS II–IV

The Author's Note with which *Dracula* begins reflects a popular conceit in eighteenth-century fiction. Rather than constructing a narrative from the perspective of an omniscient third-person narrator, Stoker presents the story through transcribed journals. In effect, the novel masquerades as a real diary. Were the story told as a first-person reflection, we would be sure of the fate of the protagonist: because he is telling his tale, he must have lived through it. However, because the author of the diary writes directly as events happen, he may be tragically unaware of the danger of his surroundings. Harker has no time to reflect on his experiences and no way of knowing if he is placing himself in danger.

This real-time technique is popular within the horror genre: since the narrator has no way of knowing how the story will end, neither does the audience. The 1999 film *The Blair Witch Project* provides an excellent example of this conceit in recent popular culture. The film purports to be the exact contents of several film reels found in a supposedly haunted Maryland forest, shortly after a documentary film team vanished there while attempting to record supernatural activity. Watching the film, we experience what the documentary filmmakers supposedly experienced, in real time, to terrifying effect.

Because contemporary readers are so familiar with the vampire legend—whether in the form of T*he Lost Boys, Buffy the Vampire Slayer, Salem's Lot*, or countless other incarnations—it is difficult to appreciate the magnitude of shock and dread that Stoker's contemporaries felt upon reading his novel. For us, the suspense more likely comes from watching the characters piece together the count's puzzle.

Chapter III contains one of the most discussed scenes in the novel. Drifting in and out of consciousness, Harker is visited by the three female vampires, who dance seductively before the angry count drives them away. The women's appearance in the room where Harker is sleeping is undeniably sexual, as the Englishman's characteristically staid language becomes suddenly ornate. Harker notes "the ruby of their voluptuous lips" and feels "a wicked, burning desire that they would kiss me." As he stretches beneath the advancing women "in an agony of delightful anticipation," his position suggests, not at all subtly, an act of oral sex:

> The fair girl . . . bent over me till I could feel the
> movement of her breath upon me. . . . The girl went on
> her knees, and bent over me, simply gloating. There was
> a deliberate voluptuousness which was both thrilling and

repulsive, and as she arched her neck she actually licked her lips like an animal. . . .

Harker is simultaneously confronting a vampire and another creature equally terrifying to Victorian England: an unabashedly sexual woman. The women's voluptuousness puts them at odds with the two English heroines, Lucy Westenra and Mina Murray, whom we see later in the novel. The fact that the vampire women prey on a defenseless child perverts any notion of maternity, further distinguishing them from their Victorian counterparts. These "weird sisters," as Van Helsing later calls them, stand as a reminder of what is perhaps Dracula's greatest threat to society: the transformation of prim, proper, and essentially sexless English ladies into uncontrollable, lustful animals.

Harker spends a lot of time wondering whether this vision of repulsion and delight is real. He is unsure whether the women actually bend closer and closer to him, or if he merely dreams of their approach. If the women are real, they threaten to drink Harker's blood, fortifying themselves by depleting his strength. If they are merely part of a fantastic dream, as Harker suspects, they nonetheless threaten to drain him of another vital fluid—semen. Critic C.F. Bentley believes that the passage in which Harker lies "in languorous ecstasy and wait[s]—wait[s] with beating heart" suggests a nocturnal emission. Either way, Harker stands to be drained of a vital fluid, which to the Victorian male imagination represents an overturning of the male-dominated social structure.

CHAPTERS V–VII

SUMMARY: CHAPTER V

Chapter V consists of several letters and a diary entry. In England, Mina Murray and her friend, Lucy Westenra, exchange letters about their respective romances. Mina is an assistant schoolmistress whose desire to be useful to her future husband has led her to study shorthand and typewriting. She happily reports that her fiancé, Jonathan Harker, has written that he is on his way home. Lucy replies with tales of her own marriage prospects. She has entertained proposals from several men, including Dr. John Seward—the director of a lunatic asylum in London—and a rich American named Quincey Morris. Her heart, however, belongs to a gentleman named Arthur Holmwood, whose proposal she has accepted.

The women's correspondence is followed by a diary entry, on phonograph, by Dr. Seward. The doctor admits his unhappiness at Lucy's rebuff, but occupies himself with an interesting new patient, a man named Renfield. Following this entry is a congratulatory letter from Quincey Morris to Arthur Holmwood.

SUMMARY: CHAPTER VI
In her journal, Mina describes her visit with Lucy in the picturesque town of Whitby, on the northeast coast of England, and the ruined abbey there that is reputed to be haunted. Mr. Swales, an elderly resident who befriends the two girls and tells them stories about the town, scoffs at such legends. Mr. Swales asserts that most of the graves in the Whitby churchyard are empty, as their supposed occupants were lost at sea. After Swales departs, Mina listens to Lucy's wedding plans and notes sadly that she has not heard from Jonathan for a month.

John Seward continues to report the curious case of Renfield in his diary. The patient has the curious habit of consuming living creatures. He uses sugar to trap flies, uses flies to trap spiders, and uses spiders to trap sparrows. He delights as one creature consumes another and believes that he himself draws strength by eating these creatures. Seward classifies Renfield as a "zoöphagous"—or life-eating—maniac who desires to "absorb as many lives as he can."

Meanwhile, Mina expresses anxiety over her missing fiancé and over Lucy, who has begun to sleepwalk during the night. Although she seems healthy, Lucy exhibits an "odd concentration" that Mina does not understand. While out walking one day, Mina encounters Mr. Swales, who tells her that he senses his own death is likely not far off. He assures her that he is not afraid of dying and that death is "all that we can rightly depend on." Mina and Mr. Swales see a ship drifting about offshore as if no one were at the helm. Guessing the vessel to be "Russian, by the look of her," Mr. Swales assures Mina that they will surely hear more about it.

SUMMARY: CHAPTER VII
Two newspaper clippings indicate that the ship Mina and Mr. Swales have seen, a vessel called the Demeter, later washes up on the shore at Whitby during a terrific storm. Its crew is nowhere to be found, while its captain, dead and clasping a crucifix, is discovered

tied to the wheel. When the ship runs aground, a huge dog leaps from the hold and disappears into the countryside. The Demeter's only cargo is a number of large wooden boxes, which are delivered to a Whitby solicitor.

Selections from the captain's log of the Demeter follow, describing the ship's voyage to England from the Russian port of Varna. The trip starts off well, but ten days into the voyage, a crewmember is found missing. Soon thereafter, another sailor spots a tall, thin man who is not like any of the crew. A search of the ship finds no stowaways, but every few days another sailor disappears. The crew becomes numb with fear, and the first mate begins to go mad. By the time the ship reaches the English coast, only four men remain to sail it. A great fog settles over them, preventing them from reaching harbor. After two more sailors vanish, the first mate goes below to find the intruder, only to rush out of the hold and throw himself into the sea. That night, in order to "baffle this fiend or monster," the captain resolves to lash himself and his crucifix to the wheel and to stay with his ship to the end.

The narrative returns to Mina's journal. Mina describes the night of the dreaded storm, her fears for Jonathan, and her concern for Lucy, who continues to sleepwalk. On the day of the sea captain's funeral, Mina reports that Lucy is increasingly restless. One reason for Lucy's agitation, Mina believes, is the recent death of Mr. Swales, who was found dead with a broken neck and a look of horror on his face.

ANALYSIS: CHAPTERS V–VII

In Gothic literature, the battle between well-defined forces of good and evil frequently dominates plots. In *Dracula*, that battle is largely waged over the fate of its female protagonists, Lucy Westenra and Mina Murray. Neither Mina nor Lucy is a particularly profound character—instead, both represent the Victorian ideal of female virtue. The two sets of women we have seen thus far in the novel stand in stark and obvious opposition to each other: Lucy and Mina represent purity and goodness, while the predatory sisters in Dracula's castle represent corruption and evil. The count threatens womanly virtue, as the frighteningly voluptuous sisters testify to his ability to transform ladies into sex-crazed "devils of the Pit."

Both Lucy and Mina face the threat of such transformation later in the novel. It is perhaps no surprise that, of the two, Lucy falls most disastrously under Dracula's spell. Although Lucy's let-ters pay homage to a certain male fantasy of domination—"My dear Mina, why are men so noble when we women are so little worthy of them?"—they also reveal that she is a sexualized being. Lucy is not only an object of desire who garners three marriage proposals in a single day, but is herself capable of desiring oth-ers. Lucy writes: "Why can't they let a girl marry three men, or as many as want her, and save all this trouble?" Though Lucy imme-diately condemns her own words as "heresy," her apology does not blot out her desire to experience life beyond the narrow con-fines of conventional morality.

Mina and Lucy's correspondence contrasts sharply with the terror-filled journal entries that comprise the first four chapters. The London society that Mina, Lucy, and Dr. Seward inhabit is marked by order, reason, and progress: Mina is a schoolmistress who occupies herself with shorthand and typewriting lessons, while Seward, ever hopeful of diagnosing and curing his mentally ill patients, records his diary entries on a newfangled phono-graph. The world that Dracula inhabits, in contrast, is ruled by the seemingly impossible or unexplainable: people neither age nor die, and men crawl down sheer walls. Dracula's foreign presence threatens to overturn the whole of Western culture by subverting carefully constructed and policed morals and by allowing super-stition to trump logic.

Lucy's and Mina's letters also introduce most of the main char-acters we see in the remainder of the novel. Lucy describes her three suitors, who are largely two-dimensional characters: Seward is a serious intellectual, Quincey Morris a slang-talking Texan, and Arthur Holmwood is a bland nobleman. Stoker is more concerned with creating a band of men whose goodness is unquestionable than with creating complex, multifaceted charac-ters. This characterization sets up a framework for a clear-cut moral battle later in the novel.

The colorful character of Mr. Swales is noteworthy for two rea-sons. First, as an unapologetic skeptic, Swales stands in contrast to the Eastern European peasants, whose lives are ruled by supersti-tions. When Mina directs their conversation to local legends, Swales responds, "It be all fool-talk, lock, stock and barrel; that's what it be, an' nowt else." Though uneducated, Swales stands as a product of Western society: he is too committed to reason to allow for the existence of "bans an' wafts an' boh-ghosts an' barguests an' bogles." Swales is also noteworthy because he exemplifies Stoker's dedication to capturing regional dialects. Van Helsing and many of the novel's secondary characters speak with heavy accents that the author transcribes carefully. But some critics have pointed out that Stoker relies less on a precise ear than on stereotype to generate his characters' dialogue. In Chapter V, for instance, Quincey's proposal to Lucy Westenra reads like a parody of the language patterns of the American South: "Miss Lucy, I know I ain't good enough to regulate the fixin's of your little shoes, but . . . won't you just hitch up alongside of me and let us go down the long road together, driving in double harness?"

Another significant character introduced in this section is Renfield, Dr. Seward's "zoöphagous" maniac. Renfield's consumption of flies, spiders, and sparrows is spurred by his belief that their lives are transferred into his own, providing him with strength and vitality. Renfield's habit mirrors the count's means of sustenance and confirms Stoker's concern with the relationship between humans and beasts. From a psychoanalytic standpoint, the desire to consume is a primal urge to incorporate an object into one's self and at the same time to destroy the object.

Largely because of the relatively recent publication of Charles Darwin's *The Origin of Species* (1859) and *The Descent of Man* (1871), Victorian society was anxious about such primal urges, seeking to keep them hidden beneath the veneers of science, art, and polite conversation. Darwin's works questioned the centuries-old belief in creationism and toppled the previously unassailable hierarchy of man over beast. Humans were no longer the undisputed crown of creation—they were merely another link in a great chain. Although the last decades of the eighteenth and first decades of the nineteenth century were ripe with scientific advancements, they were also marked by a profound sense of uneasiness at having to abandon old and refuted, but nevertheless comfortable, modes of thought. Thus, because it confirms the animalistic and possibly savage nature of human beings, Renfield's behavior would have caused no small shock among Stoker's original readers. In Seward's lunatic, we see how fine a line separates the beast from the drawing-room dandy.

Chapters VIII–IX

Summary: Chapter VIII

On August 10, Mina awakens to find Lucy's bed empty. She goes outside to find Lucy and sees her in the churchyard, reclining on her favorite bench with a dark figure bending over her. As Mina approaches, the figure looks toward her, exposing a pale face and gleaming red eyes. By the time Mina reaches Lucy, however, the figure is gone. Lucy is apparently asleep but gasping for breath, so Mina wraps her in a shawl and leads her home. When Lucy wakes, Mina finds "two little red points like pin-pricks" on her friend's neck, and decides that she must have accidentally pricked Lucy while helping her pin her shawl.

Lucy attempts to sleepwalk again the following two nights, but Mina thwarts Lucy's efforts by locking the bedroom door. Later, the two women go for a walk together. As the sun sets, they see a dark figure in the graveyard, and Lucy comments on the red glint of his eyes. That night, Mina awakes to find Lucy sitting up in bed, pointing to the window. Mina looks outside and sees a large bat fluttering in the moonlight. When she turns around, she finds Lucy sleeping peacefully. During the next few days, Lucy grows pale and haggard, and the puncture wounds at her throat grow larger. Mina worries about the well-being of her friends: about Lucy's failing health; about Lucy's mother, who is too ill to bear any anxiety over Lucy's state; and about the still-missing Jonathan Harker.

Mina's journal entry is followed by a letter from a Whitby solicitor, ordering the boxes of earth from the Demeter to be delivered to the estate of Carfax, the house Dracula has purchased. We return to Mina's diary, where she writes that Lucy's health seems to be improving. News comes that Jonathan has appeared in a Hungarian hospital in Buda-Pest, suffering from brain fever. Mina prepares to leave England to be with Jonathan.

The narrative shifts to John Seward's accounts of his patient Renfield, who has grown both violent and boastful, telling the doctor that "the Master is at hand." One night, Renfield escapes and runs to Carfax, where Dr. Seward finds him pressing against the door of the mansion's chapel, calling out to his master and promising obedience. The attendants return Renfield to his cell, where he begs his master to be patient.

SUMMARY: CHAPTER IX

Mina writes from Buda-Pest, telling Lucy that Jonathan has changed greatly. He is "a wreck of himself" and remembers nothing of his time in Transylvania. The nun tending to Jonathan confides in Mina that he often raves deliriously about unspeakable things. Jonathan is still in possession of his diary and knows that the cause of his brain fever is recorded in it. He turns the diary over to Mina, making her promise that she will never mention what is written there unless some "solemn duty" requires it. The couple decides to marry immediately, and Mina seals the diary shut with wax, promising never to open it except in a dire emergency. Lucy sends Mina a letter of congratulation.

Meanwhile, Renfield has become more docile, repeatedly mumbling, "I can wait; I can wait." A few days later, however, he escapes again and turns up once more at the door of the chapel at Carfax. When Dr. John Seward follows with his attendants, Renfield moves to attack, but grows calm at the sight of a great bat sweeping across the face of the moon.

Lucy begins a diary, in which she records bad dreams and recounts that something scratches at her window in the night. Concerned that Lucy has become pale and weak again, Arthur Holmwood writes to Dr. Seward, asking him to examine her. Seward does so, and reports that Lucy's illness is beyond his experience. He sends for his former teacher, the celebrated Professor Van Helsing of Amsterdam, to examine the girl. Van Helsing arrives, observes Lucy, and then returns home briefly, asking to be kept abreast of Lucy's condition by telegram. He tells Seward that he cannot ascertain the cause of Lucy's illness, but concurs that much of her blood has been lost.

Renfield, meanwhile, resumes his habit of catching flies. However, when the doctor comes to see Renfield at sunset, he tosses out his flies, claiming that he is "sick of all that rubbish." Lucy seems to show improvement for a few days, as Seward's telegrams to Van Helsing relate. On September 6, however, there is a terrible change for the worse, and the doctor begs his old master to come immediately.

ANALYSIS: CHAPTERS VIII–IX

Dracula's portrayal of women makes the novel seem like a fantasy of the Victorian male imagination. Women are primarily objects of delicate beauty who occasionally need to be rescued from danger—a task that, more than anything else, ends up bolstering the ego of their male saviors. Indeed, among the female characters in the novel, only Mina exercises any considerable strength or resourcefulness. The other women are primarily two-dimensional victims, pictures of perfection who are easy for Dracula to prey upon. Both Lucy and her mother are helplessly weak, and the latter is too delicate to bear even the suggestion that something is amiss with her daughter's health.

Despite the profound political and social change that crossed England in the late nineteenth century, Stoker displays little interest in the advancement of women. Though Mina brightly—albeit briefly—considers one of the promises of feminism, the novel as a whole does not align itself with her cause. In reference to Lucy's recent engagement, Mina writes,

> Some of the 'New Women' writers will some day start an idea that men and women should be allowed to see each other asleep before proposing or accepting. But I suppose the New Woman won't condescend in future to accept; she will do the proposing herself. And a nice job she will make of it, too!

While Mina herself approaches this kind of self-reliance—after all, it is her research that later leads Van Helsing's band to the count's castle—she never fully graduates into the new womanhood she describes here.

Given Stoker's obsessive concern with female chastity and virtue, it is hard to imagine him granting his female characters the degree of sexual freedom necessary to become "New Women." In fact, these chapters make the erotic nature of Dracula's attacks even more obvious. Lucy's wounds suggest a virgin's first sexual encounter: she escapes into the night and is penetrated in a way that makes her bleed. After this initial encounter, Lucy hungers for more, attempting to steal out of the house and return to the graveyard.

Although Mina does not yet realize the nature of her friend's sleepwalking excursions, she is filled with anxiety not only for Lucy's health, but also for "her reputation in case the story should get wind." Already viewed to some degree as a dangerous sexual adventurer, Lucy begins her transformation from a pure maiden into a figure of female wantonness. In this sense, Dracula threatens not merely a single girl, but also the entire moral order of the Victorian world and its ideals of sexual purity.

The epistolary form of the novel allows Stoker to maintain suspense throughout, not only keeping us in the dark, but also keeping his own characters guessing at the nature of their own predicaments. Indeed, at this point in the novel, we know much more than any one individual character does. Though we understand the implications of the shipment of earth that arrives at Carfax, Dr. Seward does not, which means he has no way to explain the increasingly drastic behavior of his patient, Renfield. Continuing with this technique and permitting the events to unfold in the present tense allows Stoker to achieve an impressive amount of suspense.

CHAPTERS X–XI

SUMMARY: CHAPTER X

Seward and Holmwood are concerned about Lucy's suddenly failing health. When Van Helsing arrives to find Lucy terribly pale and unable to breathe easily, he transfuses Holmwood's blood into Lucy. The doctors examine the punctures on Lucy's neck. Though Seward is convinced that these wounds caused her severe loss of blood, he can offer no explanation for them. Van Helsing orders Seward to stay up with Lucy that night. The young doctor does so, and Lucy awakes feeling much restored.

The following night, however, the exhausted Seward falls asleep on his watch. The next morning, he and Van Helsing find Lucy pale and completely drained of strength, her gums shrunken and her lips white. Seward performs another transfusion, this time providing the blood himself. Attempting to sleep, Seward wakes to thoughts of the punctures on Lucy's neck and the ragged appearance of their edges. That afternoon, a large package arrives for Van Helsing. It contains white garlic flowers, which Van Helsing orders Lucy to wear around her neck. Under the skeptical gaze of Seward, Van Helsing places garlic flowers all around the room and leaves Lucy, assuring Seward that she will now be able to sleep safely.

SUMMARY: CHAPTER XI

In the morning, Van Helsing and Dr. Seward return to the Westenra residence. They are greeted by Lucy's mother, who tells them that during the night she removed all the "horrible, strong-smelling flowers" from Lucy's room and opened the windows to let in fresh air. After Mrs. Westenra leaves the room, Van Helsing nearly crumbles. He and Seward rush to their patient to find her near death. Only another blood transfusion from Van Helsing resuscitates her. Van Helsing warns Mrs. Westenra never to remove anything from Lucy's room again. For the next four days all is well, and Lucy reports that she feels much better.

A clipping from the Pall Mall Gazette reports that a large wolf escaped from the Zoological Gardens. The animal returns the next morning, covered in broken glass. Seward's September 17 diary entry reports that Renfield attacks the young doctor in his office, and cuts the doctor's wrist. Renfield proceeds to lick up the blood, and repeats, over and over, the phrase, "The blood is the life!"

Van Helsing telegrams Seward that day, advising him to spend the night with Lucy, but there is a delay and the message does not arrive until the following morning. On September 17, the night of the wolf's escape, Lucy awakens, frightened by a flapping at the window and a howling outside. Mrs. Westenra is also scared by the noise and comes in and joins her daughter in bed. Suddenly, the window shatters and the head of a huge wolf appears. Terrified, Lucy's mother tears the garlic wreath from her daughter's neck and suffers a fatal heart attack. As Lucy loses consciousness, she sees the wolf draw his head back from the window. The four household maids enter, horrified by the sight of their dead mistress. The women go into the dining room to have a glass of wine, but the wine is drugged and they all pass out. Left defenseless and alone, Lucy hides her latest diary entry in her bodice, hoping that "they shall find it when they come to lay me out."

SUMMARY & ANALYSIS

ANALYSIS: CHAPTERS X–XI

Seward's inability to diagnose or stem the progression of Lucy's illness demonstrates the effectiveness of Dracula's assault on Victorian social order and also exposes the limits of Western science and reason. Only legend and superstition—not reason and science—are effective in fighting Dracula. Even the many advancements of medical science prove useless. Maintaining an open mind and acknowledging the power of superstition, Van Helsing challenges the rigorous confines of Victorian thought. Although Van Helsing proves himself a competent modern surgeon by performing one blood transfusion after another, neither his methods nor his knowledge are restricted to the teachings of Western medicine. As he places garlic flowers around Lucy's room, he steps outside the role of doctor and becomes more of a "philosopher and a metaphysician." One of the main ironies of the novel is that the Londoners are made vulnerable to Dracula's attacks precisely because they live in a world that encourages them to dismiss such supernatural predators as powerless in a civilized society such as Britain.

Though Lucy's blood transfusions occur so frequently as to seem almost comical, they serve two important metaphorical functions. First, the transfusions confirm the moral purity of the men who submit to them for Lucy's sake. If there were ever any doubt about the moral righteousness of Van Helsing and his compatriots, Stoker means to dispel it here. The blood itself is characterized as morally outstanding: preparing Holmwood for the first transfusion, Van Helsing points out that his patient "is so young and strong and of blood so pure that we need not defibrinate it."

Second, the transfusions hint at a kind of sexual intimacy that societal constraints prevented Stoker from writing about openly in the 1890s. The transfer of the men's blood into Lucy's veins has physiological effects similar to those of sexual intercourse: afterward, the men feel spent, but the act brings a revitalized flush of color to Lucy's cheek. More important, the characters themselves suggest a parallel between the two acts. Van Helsing not only says that it might be improper for Arthur to learn that other men have donated their blood to his fiancée, but also makes a direct connection between blood and sexuality: "No man knows, till he experiences it, what it is to feel his own life-blood drawn away into the veins of the woman he loves."

Van Helsing's comments could well be the words a popular romance novelist rather than a medical professional. However, the link Van Helsing makes is crucial to establishing the scope of Dracula's threat. As Dracula repeatedly drains Lucy of her transfused blood, he comes to possess not only Lucy's body, but also the bodies of all the men who have offered her their blood. In this way, the count begins to make good on his threat to the three weird sisters in Chapter III—if his power goes unchecked, all of these men will indeed "belong to [him]."

CHAPTERS XII–XIV

SUMMARY: CHAPTER XII

The narrative returns to Seward's diary entries. Arriving at the Westenras' the next day, Van Helsing and Seward find the scene of destruction: the maids unconscious on the dining room floor, Mrs. Westenra dead, and Lucy once again at death's door, with terrible, mangled wounds at her neck. Neither of the men can spare any more blood, but Lucy's third suitor, Quincey Morris, appears and agrees to take part in a transfusion. Puzzled, Morris asks what has become of all the blood that has already been transferred to Lucy. Holmwood arrives. His father's recent death, combined with the loss of Mrs. Westenra and Lucy's failing health, nearly makes him despondent, but his presence helps rally his fiancée's spirits.

Unaware of what has befallen Lucy, Mina writes a letter informing Lucy that she and Jonathan have married and have returned to England. Dr. Seward's assistant writes to tell him that Renfield escaped again and attacked two men carrying boxes of earth from Carfax. Van Helsing surrounds his dying patient with garlic, but she pushes the flowers away as she sleeps. When Seward checks on Lucy during the night, he notices a bat hovering near her window. On the morning of September 20, the wounds on Lucy's neck disappear. Sensing that Lucy is nearing the end of her life, the doctors awaken Holmwood and bring him to say good-bye. In a strangely seductive voice, Lucy begs Holmwood to kiss her, but Van Helsing pulls him away, instructing him to kiss Lucy only on the forehead. Holmwood complies with Van Helsing's instructions, and Lucy dies, recovering in death the beauty that she lost during her long illness.

SUMMARY: CHAPTER XIII

Seward's diary continues, as he describes Lucy's burial. Before the funeral, Van Helsing covers the coffin and body with garlic and places a crucifix in Lucy's mouth. He tells a confused Seward that after the funeral, they must cut off Lucy's head and take out her heart. The next day, however, Van Helsing discovers that someone has stolen the crucifix from the body and tells Seward that they will have to wait before doing anything more. The heartbroken Holmwood—referred to as Lord Godalming since his father's death—turns to Seward for consolation. Looking at Lucy's unnaturally lovely corpse, Holmwood cannot believe she is really dead. Van

Helsing asks Holmwood for Lucy's personal papers, hoping that they will provide some clue as to the cause of her death.

Meanwhile, Mina writes in her diary that in London she and Jonathan have seen a tall, fierce man with a black mustache and beard. Jonathan is convinced the man is Count Dracula. Jonathan becomes so upset that he slips into a deep sleep and remembers nothing when he wakes. Mina decides that, for the sake of her husband's health, she must read his diary entries from his time in Transylvania.

That night, Mina receives a telegram informing her of Lucy's death. This message is followed by an excerpt from a local paper, which reports that a number of children have been temporarily abducted in Hampstead Heath—the area where Lucy was buried—by a strange woman whom the children call the "Bloofer Lady." When the children return home, they bear strange wounds on their necks.

SUMMARY: CHAPTER XIV

Transcribing her husband's journal, Mina is horrified by its contents. When Van Helsing visits Mina in order to discuss the events leading up to Lucy's death, she is so impressed that she gives him Jonathan's diary to read. Van Helsing reads the diary and returns to see the couple at breakfast the next day. Van Helsing's belief in Jonathan's observations restores the young man's memories of his time in Transylvania. Realizing that Dracula must indeed have journeyed to England, Harker begins a new diary.

Seward reports that Renfield has returned to his habit of catching flies and spiders. Van Helsing visits the young doctor and points out the newspaper accounts of the "Bloofer Lady," taking care to note that the abducted children always reappear with wounds on their necks similar to those that appeared on Lucy's neck. Seward is skeptical of any connection, but his mentor urges him to believe in the possibility of the supernatural—of occurrences that cannot be explained by reason. Van Helsing suddenly concludes that it must be Lucy who is responsible for the marks on the children's necks.

ANALYSIS: CHAPTERS XII–XIV

In this section, we witness Lucy's transformation into a supernatural creature. The description of her death immediately alerts us that she has crossed into the realm of the supernatural: the wounds on her neck disappear and all of her "loveliness [comes] back to her in death." The clippings about the threatening "Bloofer Lady" make it clear that Lucy has indeed become a vampire. Dracula's attack has transformed a model of English chastity and purity into an openly sexual predator. When Holmwood visits Lucy for the last time, her physical appeal startles him: "she looked her best, with all the soft lines matching the angelic beauty of her eyes." Equally startling is the newfound forwardness with which she demands sexual satisfaction: "Arthur! Oh, my love, I am so glad you have come! Kiss me!" Dracula's power has indeed topped one former example of the Victorian female ideal.

Lucy's body also becomes a metaphorical battleground between the forces of good and evil, between the forces for liberation and repression of female sexuality. While Dracula fights for control of Lucy, through whom he believes he can access many Englishmen, Van Helsing's crew pumps her full of brave men's blood, which they believe is the "best thing on this earth when a woman is in trouble." This battle reflects the struggle of Victorian society to recognize and accept female sexuality. Victorian England prized women for their docility and domesticity, leaving them no room for open expression of sexual desire, even within the confines of marriage. Mina, though married, appears no less chaste than Lucy. This obsession with purity was pervasive: less than twenty years before the publication of *Dracula*, medical authorities still believed that a menstruating woman could spoil meat simply by touching it.

Van Helsing articulates these prejudices of the Victorian age as he praises Mina's character, saying:

> She is one of God's women, fashioned by His own hand to show us men and other women that there is a heaven where we can enter, and that its light can be here on earth. So true, so sweet, so noble, so little an egoist—and that, let me tell you, is much in this age, so skeptical and selfish."

Van Helsing's statement implies that a woman who cannot manage this much truth, sweetness, nobility, and modesty has no place in Victorian society. Though Lucy possesses all of these in plenty, she also betrays a fatal flaw: her openness to sexual adventure. Recalling Van Helsing's lesson in vampire lore, we know that Dracula is powerless to enter a home unless invited. The count thus would not have been able to access Lucy's bedroom unless she invited him in.

Though no character ever blames Lucy for her susceptibility to seduction—or even mentions it—we are aware that the young woman has fallen from grace. Victorian society firmly dictated that wantonness came at a high price, and in Dracula, Lucy pays dearly.

CHAPTERS XV–XVIII

SUMMARY: CHAPTER XV

Seward is appalled by Van Helsing's suggestion that Lucy is in some way responsible for the rash of wounded children. However, due to his respect for the elder doctor, he accompanies Van Helsing on his investigation. The two men visit one of the wounded children and find that the marks on the child's neck are identical to Lucy's. That night, Seward and Van Helsing proceed to Lucy's tomb, open the coffin, and find it empty. Seward suggests that a grave robber might have taken the corpse, but Van Helsing instructs him to keep watch at one side of the churchyard.

Near dawn, Seward witnesses a "white streak" moving between the trees. He and Van Helsing approach and find a child lying nearby, but Seward still refuses to believe that Lucy is responsible for any wrongdoing. Only after they return to Lucy's tomb, finding her restored to her coffin and "radiantly beautiful," does Seward feel the "horrid sense of the reality of things." Van Helsing explains that Lucy belongs to the "Un-Dead" and insists that she must be decapitated, her mouth filled with garlic, and a stake driven through her heart. The two men meet with Arthur Holmwood and Quincey Morris, and Van Helsing explains what must be done. Holmwood is opposed to mutilating his fiancée's corpse, but finally agrees to accompany them to the graveyard.

SUMMARY: CHAPTER XVI

That night, the four men go to Lucy's grave and find it empty. Van Helsing seals the door of the tomb with Communion wafers to prevent the vampire Lucy from reentering. The men then hide in wait. Eventually, a figure appears, dressed entirely in white and carrying a child. It is Lucy—or rather, a monster that looks like Lucy, with eyes "unclean and full of hell-fire" and a mouth stained with fresh blood. As the men surround her, she drops the child and calls out passionately to Holmwood, telling him to come to her. Holmwood begins to move, but Van Helsing leaps between the couple and brandishes a crucifix. Lucy recoils. Van Helsing quickly removes the Communion wafers, and the vampire slips through the door of her tomb.

Having witnessed this horror, Holmwood concurs that the necessary rites must be performed, and the following evening, he returns to hammer a stake through Lucy's heart. As Lucy returns to a state of beauty, Van Helsing reassures Holmwood that he has saved Lucy's soul from eternal darkness and has given her peace at last. Before leaving the tomb, Van Helsing makes plans to reunite with the men two nights later, so that they may discuss the "terrible task" before them.

SUMMARY: CHAPTER XVII

At Van Helsing's urging, Jonathan and Mina Harker come to stay with Seward at the asylum. Mina transcribes Seward's diary with the typewriter and notes its account of Lucy's death. Meanwhile, Seward reads the Harkers' journals, realizing for the first time that Dracula may well be his next-door neighbor and that there may be a connection between the vampire's proximity and Renfield's behavior. The lunatic Renfield is calm at the moment, and Seward wonders what this tranquility indicates about Dracula's whereabouts.

Meanwhile, Jonathan researches the boxes of earth that were shipped from Transylvania to England. He discovers that all fifty were delivered to the chapel at Carfax, but worries that some might have been moved elsewhere in recent weeks. Mina notes that Harker seems to have fully recovered from his ordeal in Transylvania. Holmwood and Morris arrive at the asylum, and, clearly, Holmwood is still terribly shaken by Lucy's death.

SUMMARY: CHAPTER XVIII

With Seward's permission, Mina visits Renfield. The madman frantically swallows his collection of flies and spiders before she enters, but is extremely polite and seems rational in her presence. Van Helsing arrives at the asylum. Pleased to see that Seward's diaries and letters have been typed and placed in order, he compliments Mina on her work but hopes that she will be spared a role in the business before them. The destruction of the vampire, he notes, is "no part for a woman."

Van Helsing gathers the entire company and tells them the legend of the nosferatu, or "Un-Dead." He says that such creatures are immortal and immensely strong; have command over various animals and the elements; and can vanish and change form at will.

However, they also have certain weaknesses: they cannot survive without blood; cannot enter a house unless summoned; lose their power at daybreak, at which time they must seek shelter in the earth or a coffin; and are powerless before crucifixes, Communion wafers, and other holy objects. To kill Dracula, Van Helsing says they must first track down his fifty boxes of earth. He also resolves that Mina must not be burdened with or endangered by the details of their work. The men tell Mina that they "are men and are able to bear; but you must be our star and our hope."

The entire company asks to see Renfield. They gather, and he makes a remarkably rational and passionate plea to be released at once in order to avoid terrible consequences. Fearing that this sudden display of sanity is but "another form or phase of his madness," Seward denies Renfield's request.

Analysis: Chapters XV–XVIII

In this section, Lucy's transformation reaches its terrible end. Lucy is now a perversion of the two most sacred female virtues in Victorian England: maternalism and sexual purity. In Chapter XVII, Mina voices an expectation of Victorian culture when she writes, "We women have something of the mother in us that makes us rise above smaller matters when the mother-spirit is invoked." Like the three women Harker meets in Dracula's castle, the undead Lucy counters this "mother-spirit" by preying on innocent children. Rather than providing them with nourishment and protection, she stalks and feeds on them. The hideous transformation of this once beautiful woman into a demonic child-killer demonstrates the anxiety the Victorians felt about women whose sexual behavior challenged convention.

Van Helsing's band of do-gooders feels this same anxiety about female sexuality as they face off against its hypersexualized opponent. As the men confront Lucy, whose purity has changed to "voluptuous wantonness," we note the rather limited vocabulary Stoker uses to paint the scene. Lucy is described almost exclusively in terms of her sexuality: her face becomes "wreathed with a voluptuous smile," and she advances with "outstretched arms and a wanton smile." Lucy's words to Holmwood echo her dying wish for his kiss: "Come to me, Arthur. . . . My arms are hungry for you. Come, and we can rest together. Come, my husband, come!" Her words are both a plea for and a promise of sexual satisfaction. Van

Helsing and his crew's response to Lucy's words illustrate that the men are certainly aware of the words' double meaning. The men are equally attracted to and horrified by the woman who would make such a bold proposition: "There was something diabolically sweet in her tones . . . which rang through the brains even of us who heard the words addressed to another. As for Arthur, he seemed under a spell; moving his hands from his face, he opened wide his arms." Dracula's power is indeed considerable, as it tempts even morally righteous men who are aware of the count's diabolical plans.

Tempted as the men are by Lucy's carnal embrace, they are equally eager to destroy her. Throughout the descriptions of Lucy's voluptuousness runs a strong indication of the men's desire to annihilate her. Dr. Seward writes, "[T]he remnant of my love passed into hate and loathing; had she then to be killed, I could have done it with savage delight." Having paid for sexual curiosity with her eternal soul, Lucy must now pay an equally steep price for her sexual appetite.

The act of Lucy's final destruction strongly resembles an act of sexual congress. Holmwood's piercing of Lucy with his stake unmistakably suggests intercourse: her body "shook and quivered and twisted in wild contortions. . . . But Arthur never faltered . . . driving deeper and deeper the mercy-bearing stake." Holmwood's attack restores Lucy's purity and soul, thus implying that Holmwood returns Lucy to the socially desirable state of monogamy and submission. As her fiancé, Holmwood cleanses the "carnal and unspiritual" from Lucy by consummating a sexual relationship that, without Dracula's interference, would have not only been consecrated by God, but also would have legitimized Lucy's troublesome sexual desires.

CHAPTERS XIX–XXI

SUMMARY: CHAPTER XIX

The men make the journey to Carfax, arming themselves with holy objects for protection. There is no sign of Dracula in the chapel, but there is a terrible stench, and the men find twenty-nine of the original fifty boxes of earth. To the men's horror, rats begin to fill the chapel. The men use a whistle to summon dogs that chase away the rats. Van Helsing's spirits are high despite the fact that twenty-one boxes are missing. Upon returning to the asylum, Van Helsing asks to see Renfield again. Hoping to use the lunatic as a source of information, Van Helsing attempts an interview. Renfield curses Van Helsing and refuses to cooperate.

Mina records her mounting anxieties in her diary. One night in the asylum, she wakes up after hearing strange sounds from Renfield's room and finds that her window is open even though she is certain she closed it. Mina stares out the window at a thin streak of white mist that slowly creeps across the yard toward the asylum, seeming to have a "sentience and a vitality of its own." Mina sleeps fitfully and wakes to find a "pillar of cloud" in her room. She sees a "livid white face" bending over her, but assumes this figure is merely part of her dream.

SUMMARY: CHAPTER XX

Harker's investigations reveal that twelve of the remaining boxes of earth were deposited in two houses in London. He traces the remaining nine boxes to a house in Piccadilly, a London suburb. Harker's companions worry over how they will manage to break into a house in such a highly populated area.

Seward chronicles rapid changes in Renfield's behavior. The patient seems to have given up his interest in zoöphagy, but reiterates his earlier desire, saying, "Life is all I want." Seward questions Renfield, asking him how he accounts for the souls of the lives he plans to collect. Renfield becomes agitated at the inquiry, claiming that he has enough to worry about without thinking of souls. Seward concludes that his patient dreads the consequences of his life-gathering hobbies, which burden his soul. The following evening, the asylum attendants hear a scream and find Renfield lying in his cell, covered in blood.

SUMMARY: CHAPTER XXI

Dying, Renfield admits to the other men that Dracula often visited him, promising him flies, spiders, and other living creatures from which to gain strength in return for Renfield's obedience. Later, when Mina visited him, Renfield noted her paleness and realized that Dracula had been "taking the life out of her." He grew angry, and when the count slipped into his room that night, Renfield attempted to seize him. The vampire's eyes "burned" him, and he was flung violently across the room as Dracula slipped away into the asylum.

The four men rush upstairs to the Harkers' room. Finding it locked, they break down the door on a terrible scene: Jonathan lies unconscious, Mina kneels on the edge of the bed, and the count stands over her as she drinks from a wound on his breast. Dracula turns on the intruders, his eyes flaming with "devilish passion," but Van Helsing holds up a sacred Communion wafer and the count retreats. The moonlight fades, and the men light a gas lamp. All that is left of the count is a faint vapor escaping under the door. Morris chases it and sees a bat flying away from Carfax. Meanwhile, the men discover that the count has torn apart their study in an attempt to destroy their papers and diaries. Fortunately, they have kept duplicate copies in a safe.

Mina and Jonathan regain consciousness. Mina says that she awoke that night to find Jonathan unconscious beside her and Dracula stepping out of a mist. The count threatened to kill her husband if Mina made a sound. He drank blood from her throat, telling her that it was not the first time he had done so. Then, slicing his own chest open, he pressed her lips to the cut and forced her to drink his blood. Dracula mocked his pursuers and assured Mina that he would make her "flesh of my flesh." Mina cries out, "God pity me! Look down on a poor soul in worse than mortal peril!"

ANALYSIS: CHAPTERS XIX–XXI

In these chapters, Mina stands ready as the count's next victim. When she writes that "sleep begins to flirt with me," we know that it is Dracula—not sleep—that is seducing her during the night. These suspicions are confirmed in Chapter XXI, when, in one of the novel's strangest and most debated scenes, Van Helsing's crew barges in upon Dracula's feeding frenzy. The scene, which likely shocks us as much as it does the men, challenges gender conventions in several ways. First, neither of the men appears to be the aggressor. Rather than jumping to his wife's defense, Harker sprawls on the bed, while Dracula, rather than feeding, is fed upon. Although the count forces her into the position, Mina is in effect the instigator as she actively sucks from the wound on Dracula's chest. Here, the vampire presents a perverse mockery of the nursing mother: rather than giving life by offering milk, the count tries to ensure Mina's death by feeding her his blood. Symbols commonly viewed as male become female, and vice versa: aggression becomes stupor, and milk is transformed into blood. The entire scene defies gender categories, which would be especially troubling to Victorian audiences who relied upon rigid categories to structure their lives. In a world governed by reason and order, Dracula can pose no greater threat than by disordering gender roles.

The feeding ritual in Harker's room perverts not only the image of a mother nursing her child, but also the image of the Eucharist. The Christian ritual of Communion celebrates Christ's sacrifice through the ingestion of symbolic flesh and blood. Participation in the Eucharist, some believe, confers immortal life after death. Dracula, in contrast, consumes real—not symbolic—blood. Though the blood grants the count immortality, his soul is barred from achieving anything that resembles Christian grace. Renfield, who lives according to Dracula's philosophy, goes so far as to discredit the notion of a soul. Indeed, according to Dr. Seward's diary, the patient "dreads the consequence—the burden of a soul." Much of Van Helsing's arsenal against the count comes from Catholic symbolism, including the crucifix and holy Communion wafers. Given the rising religious skepticism in Victorian society—as Darwin's theory of evolution complicated universal acceptance of religious dogma—Stoker's novel advocates a return to the more superficial, symbolic comforts and protections of the church. Stoker suggests that a nation that ignores religion and devotes itself solely to scientific inquiry dooms itself to unimaginable spiritual dangers.

CHAPTERS XXII–XXV

SUMMARY: CHAPTER XXII

In his journal, Harker recounts the end of Renfield's story: before escaping the asylum, the count pays one last visit to the lunatic, breaking his neck and killing him. Harker and his compatriots go to Carfax the next day and place a Communion wafer in each of Dracula's boxes of earth, rendering them unfit for the vampire's habitation. Before the men proceed to the count's estate in Piccadilly, Van Helsing seals Mina Murray's room with wafers. When he touches her forehead with a wafer, it burns her skin and leaves a bright red scar on her forehead. Mina breaks down in tears, calling herself "unclean."

Summary: Chapter XXIII

The men obtain keys to Dracula's other houses around the city. Holmwood and Morris hurry off to sterilize the twelve boxes that are stored in London, while Harker and Van Helsing leave to do the same to the boxes in Piccadilly. Reaching Piccadilly, the men find only eight boxes—the ninth is missing. Mina sends a message that Dracula has left Carfax, and the men anticipate that he will soon arrive at Piccadilly in an attempt to protect his boxes. The men lie in wait, and Dracula arrives. As it is daytime, however, the count is largely powerless. Van Helsing's crew attempts an ambush, but Dracula leaps out a window and escapes.

Despite Dracula's taunts, Van Helsing believes that the count is probably frightened, knowing that he has only one box remaining as a safe resting place. Van Helsing hypnotizes Mina in an attempt to trace Dracula's movements. Under the trance, Mina's unholy connection to the count enables her spirit to be with him. Mina hears the telltale noises of sea travel, which indicates that the count has fled England by sea. Jonathan records his fears that Dracula may elude them, lying hidden for many years while Mina slowly transforms into a vampire.

Summary: Chapter XXIV

Van Helsing's band discovers that the count has boarded a ship named the Czarina Catherine, which is bound for Varna, the same Russian port from which Dracula sailed three months before. Van Helsing delivers an impassioned speech in which he declares it necessary to defeat Dracula for the good of humankind. He claims that the group "pledged to set the world free."

Van Helsing notes the effect that the "[b]aptism of blood" has had on Mina and insists that she should not be troubled with or further compromised by their hunt for the count. The men make plans to intercept Dracula in Varna, and Mina insists on accompanying them, saying that her telepathic connection to Dracula may aid their search. Van Helsing concedes, and Harker departs to make the necessary travel arrangements.

Summary: Chapter XXV

Before departing, Mina asks the group to pledge that they will, for the sake of her soul, destroy her if should she transform into a vampire. The men take a solemn vow to comply with Mina's wishes. On October 12, they board the Orient Express and make their way to

Varna, where Van Helsing arranges to board the Czarina Catherine immediately after its arrival in port.

As the days pass, Mina grows weaker. After more than a week of waiting in Varna, the band receives word that Dracula's ship has bypassed Varna and docked in the port of Galatz instead. As they prepare to board a train to Galatz, Van Helsing suggests that Mina's connection to Dracula may have enabled the count to learn of their ambush. Van Helsing insists that they not lose hope, however, reasoning that the count is now confident that he has eluded them and will not expect any further pursuit.

ANALYSIS: CHAPTERS XXII–XXV

When the Communion wafer singes Mina's forehead, the fight against Dracula's evil takes on added meaning. The men decide that their efforts also represent a fight to restore a woman to her unpolluted, virtuous self. From the beginning of the novel, Mina has proven herself resourceful and dedicated, sticking by both Jonathan and Lucy through their illnesses and faithfully transcribing journal entries in hopes of revealing the path to Dracula. Nonetheless, Mina never truly emerges as a complex or particularly believable character. Stoker's guiding principle in his characterization of Mina is not realism, but idealism. In Mina, Stoker means to create the model of Victorian female virtue. As contemporary readers, we are likely to find fault when Harker says, "Mina is sleeping now, calmly and sweetly like a little child. Her lips are curved and her face beams with happiness. Thank God, there are such moments still for her." Harker's words liken his wife to a helpless infant, whose greatest contribution to the world is merely a peaceful countenance.

The prejudices of the Victorian age partly account for Stoker's reduction of his female characters to mere bundles of virtue. There is another reason for Mina's two-dimensionality, however—one that is articulated by Dracula himself. Confronted by Van Helsing and his eager hunters, the count explains the planned course of his revenge, declaring, "Your girls that you all love are mine already; and through them you and others shall yet be mine." This statement describes the full scope of the threat Dracula presents. Van Helsing and company are not fighting for Mina's soul because they respect female purity in some abstract form, but because Dracula's influence over English women gives him direct access to both the minds and bodies of English men.

This threat explains the violence that the men—and even Mina—feel is justified in protecting themselves from the count's spell. Mina urges her comrades to kill her should she slip irretrievably into a demonic and soulless state. Mina's words—"Think, dear, that there have been times when brave men have killed their wives and their womenkind, to keep them from falling into the hands of the enemy"—attempt to explain away a link between male supremacy and violence against women. Men are justified in killing women to preserve their sense of ownership and their conception of female virtue. With the promise of this power in hand, men can rest assured of the patriarchal order of their society and of their own future control.

These chapters, marked by Dracula's flight across Europe, indicate a shift of power in the novel: the tables have turned on the count, leaving him on the defensive. The destruction of his resting places exposes Dracula's greatest weakness, forcing him to flee back to Transylvania. This flight stands as an important though temporary victory, indicating that the count's attempt to feed upon the English population has failed. For a time, it seems that Van Helsing's band will capture Dracula quickly. However, his deceptive landing at Galatz enables him to elude his pursuers—a reminder that, despite his weaknesses, the count remains formidable.

Chapters XXVI–XXVII

Summary: Chapter XXVI

Seward writes a diary entry while on the train from Varna to Galatz. He notes that Mina's trances reveal less and less, but are still of some value. Mina hears the sound of lapping water, so the band knows that Dracula remains somewhere close to water. The men hope to reach Galatz before the box is unloaded, but they are too late. The captain of the Czarina Catherine informs them that a businessman named Immanuel Hildesheim picked up the box and passed it on to a trader named Petrof Skinsky. Shortly thereafter, Skinsky's body is found in a graveyard with his throat torn out.

After Mina investigates the possible routes that the count could take to return to his castle, the band splits up and spreads out. Mina and Van Helsing take a train; Holmwood and Harker hire a steamboat; and Seward and Morris travel across the countryside on horseback. Van Helsing hastens toward Dracula's castle, hoping to purify the place before the count's arrival.

During their journey up the river, Jonathan and Arthur hear of a large, double-crewed boat ahead of them and decide this vessel must be Dracula's mode of transport. Seward and Morris rush on with their horses. Meanwhile, Mina records that she and Van Helsing have reached the town of Veresti, where they are forced to take a horse and carriage the rest of the way to the castle. Mina thus travels through the same beautiful country that her husband sees on his journey months before.

SUMMARY: CHAPTER XXVII

Van Helsing pens a memorandum to Seward, writing that he and Mina have reached the Borgo Pass. As they climb the trail toward the castle, Van Helsing finds that he can no longer hypnotize Mina. That night, fearing for her safety, he encircles her with a ring of crumbled holy Communion wafers. The three female vampires who visit Harker months before reappear. They try to tempt Van Helsing and Mina to come with them and literally frighten the horses to death.

Van Helsing leaves Mina asleep within the circle of holy wafers and proceeds on foot, reaching the castle the next afternoon. He finds the tombs of the three female vampires and is nearly paralyzed by their beauty, but forces himself to perform the rituals necessary to destroy them. Van Helsing then finds a tomb "more lordly than all the rest . . . [and] nobly proportioned." The tomb is inscribed with Dracula's name, and the professor cleanses it with the Communion wafers. Finally, he seals the castle doors with wafers to forever deny the count entry.

Mina and Van Helsing leave the castle and travel east, hoping to meet the others. There is a heavy snowfall, and wolves howl all around them. At sunset they see a large cart on the road below them, driven by Gypsies and loaded with a box of earth. From a remote location, Mina and Van Helsing watch Seward, Morris, Harker, and Holmwood close in on the Gypsies. With the sun rapidly sinking, the men intercept the cart, and the Gypsies move to defend their cargo. Harker and Morris muster incredible strength and force their way onto the cart. Harker flings the box to the ground, and Morris is wounded, but together they manage to pry open the lid. Seward and Holmwood aim their rifles at the Gypsies.

From her vantage point, Mina sees Dracula's hateful expression turn to a look of triumph. At that moment, however, Harker slashes through Dracula's throat just as Morris plunges his knife into the count's heart. Dracula dies, and as his body crumbles to dust, Mina notes in his face "a look of peace, such as I never could have imagined might have rested there." Morris is fatally wounded, but before he dies he points out that the scar has vanished from Mina's forehead.

A brief coda follows, written by Harker seven years later. He and Mina have a son named Quincey, and both Seward and Holmwood are happily married.

ANALYSIS: CHAPTERS XXVI–XXVII

Stoker reiterates the threat of rampant female sexuality by reintroducing the three vampire women who threaten to seduce Harker in the novel's opening chapters. The women pose two distinct threats. First, they stand ready to convert Mina, sapping her of her virtue and transforming her into a soulless vixen. Second, the women threaten to undermine men's reason and, by extension, the surety with which they rule the world. As Van Helsing faces the voluptuously beautiful vampires, he is nearly paralyzed with the desire to love and protect them: "She was so fair to look on, so radiantly beautiful, so exquisitely voluptuous, that the very instinct of man in me, which calls some of my sex to love and to protect one of hers, made my head whirl with new emotion." Even the righteous and pious doctor is susceptible to the vampires' diabolical temptation.

In these final chapters, we see a number of opposing forces meet for final battle. These oppositions include not merely a conflict between Victorian propriety and moral laxity, but also one between East and West, and one between Christian faith and godless magic. The Gypsies who escort Dracula's casket to his castle represent the powerful and mysterious forces of the East, of a land ruled not by science and economics but by traditions and powerful superstitions. Determined to defend the vampire against these Western invaders, the Gypsies are part of a landscape that is dark, foreign, and nearly ungovernable to the English. Storms and wolves bedevil Mina and Van Helsing as they make their way to the count's lair, and the professor loses his power to hypnotize Mina.

Despite the hostility of the landscape and its natives, the invasion is successful. Van Helsing is able to cleanse Dracula's castle and kill the three vampire women, returning them to an eternal state of purity and innocence. Stoker creates considerable drama and suspense when the band finally catches up to the count in the novel's final pages. With the terrifying sunset ominously approaching, the Englishmen's success hinges on a matter of seconds. They race against time, emerging victorious only after great effort and mortal sacrifice.

As Dracula dies, Mina notices a look of peace steal over his face. This moment in the novel speaks to one of Stoker's overarching ideas, that of Christian redemption. Though *Dracula* can be discussed endlessly as a novel of Victorian anxieties, it is also a novel of Christian propaganda. It strictly adheres to Christian doctrine, which offers eternal salvation for those who have cleansed themselves of evil. Worrying that her scar will bar her from receiving God's grace, Mina prays, "I am unclean in His eyes, and shall be until He may deign to let me stand forth in His sight as one of those who have not incurred His wrath." In this prayer, Mina voices the wish of each of the other members of the band, whose struggle has been one of good against evil in an orthodox Christian context.

The short coda, which describes how the documents have been arranged, mirrors the Author's Note that opens the novel. It is designed to reinforce a feeling of authenticity, assuring us that the events we have read are a matter of documented historical fact rather than fiction. In this way, Stoker hopes to bridge the gap between the real and the fictional, the natural and the supernatural worlds.

Important Quotations
Explained

1.   The castle is on the very edge of a terrible precipice. A stone falling from the window would fall a thousand feet without touching anything! As far as the eye can reach is a sea of green tree tops, with occasionally a deep rift where there is a chasm. Here and there are silver threads where the rivers wind in deep gorges through the forests.

    But I am not in heart to describe beauty, for when I had seen the view I explored further; doors, doors, doors everywhere, and all locked and bolted. In no place save from the windows in the castle walls is there an available exit.

    The castle is a veritable prison, and I am a prisoner!

Taken from the end of Chapter II, this passage exemplifies the dark and ominous tone Stoker creates in the novel. The tone of Harker's journal changes with amazing rapidity as his stay in Castle Dracula progresses. In the course of a single chapter, Harker feels stripped of the robes of honored houseguest and considers himself bound like a prisoner. Here, Stoker demonstrates his mastery of the conventions of the Gothic novel: evoking the ruined castle, the beautiful but overpowering landscape, and the mounting sense of dread. Though Stoker did not invent Dracula or vampire lore, he did more to solidify it in the imaginations of English-speaking audiences than any author has since. Passages such as this description have spawned countless imitators, and scores of horror films owe a debt to the simple but powerful repetition of Stoker's "doors, doors, doors everywhere."

2. I was afraid to raise my eyelids, but looked out and saw perfectly under the lashes. The girl went on her knees, and bent over me, simply gloating. There was a deliberate voluptuousness which was both thrilling and repulsive, and as she arched her neck, she actually licked her lips like an animal. . . . Lower and lower went her head as the lips went below the range of my mouth and chin and seemed about to fasten on my throat. . . . I closed my eyes in a languorous ecstasy and waited—waited with beating heart.

Things go from bad to worse rather quickly during Harker's stay with the count. In this passage from Chapter III, three beautiful vampires visit the Englishman and come dangerously close to draining him of his blood before Dracula halts them, claiming that Harker belongs to him. This passage establishes the vital link between vampirism and sex that pervades the novel. These undead women are unlike any of the living women in the novel. Whereas Mina and Lucy are models of virtue and purity, these "weird sisters" are voluptuous, aggressive, and insatiable. The position that the vampire assumes over Harker's body suggests a sexual act, and this display of female sexual aggression both attracts and repulses Harker. In a Victorian society that prizes and rewards female virginity and domesticity, the sexually adventurous vixen is bound to be the subject of fantasy. But because of these same rigid strictures of acceptable social behavior, she is also bound to be considered dangerous. Here, Stoker takes the fantasy of the dangerous whore to its most extreme manifestation, suggesting that Harker stands to lose not simply his reputation, but also his life.

3.   You are a clever man, friend John; you reason well,
        and your wit is bold; but you are too prejudiced. . . .
        Ah, it is the fault of our science that it wants to
        explain all; and if it explain not, then it says there is
        nothing to explain. But yet we see around us every day
        the growth of new beliefs, which think themselves
        new; and which are yet but the old, which pretend to
        be young. . . .

Here, in Chapter XIV, Van Helsing criticizes his protégé, Seward, for being too parochial in his attempts to diagnose Lucy. Van Helsing suggests that Seward is blinded by his own reason: if reason cannot explain a phenomenon, the young doctor tends to dismiss the phenomenon rather than question the limits of his own knowledge. Van Helsing encourages Seward to open his mind to experiences that may initially seem to counter Western methodologies. In doing so, he speaks to one of the novel's primary concerns: the consequences of modernity. In Dracula, Stoker suggests that the English find themselves preyed upon precisely because their modern knowledge, instead of enlightening them, actually prevents them from identifying the true nature of their predator. Modernity—particularly the advancements of science—has blinded the English to the dangers from which their abandoned traditions and superstitions once guarded them. Van Helsing, the only character who prizes the knowledge of both the new and the old world, advocates a brand of knowledge that incorporates the teachings of both.

QUOTATIONS

4. She still advanced, however, and with a languorous, voluptuous grace, said:—"Come to me, Arthur. Leave these others and come to me. My arms are hungry or you. Come, and we can rest together. Come, my husband, come!"

There was something diabolically sweet in her tones—something of the tingling of glass when struck-which rang through the brains even of us who heard the words addressed to another. As for Arthur, he seemed under a spell; moving his hands from his face, he opened wide his arms.

In this passage from Chapter XVI, we see one of Dracula's earlier threats made good. Earlier in the novel, the count warns his pursuers that he will defeat them by first seducing their wives and fiancées: "Your girls that you all love are mine already; and through them you and others shall yet be mine." This threat becomes reality here, as Lucy, now a blood- and sex-starved vampire, does her best to lure her fiancé, Holmwood, into eternal damnation. Like the "weird sisters" who attempt to seduce Harker, Lucy exudes sexual energy, and her words to Arthur ring out like a plea for and promise of sexual gratification. The promise proves more than Arthur can bear—"he seemed to move under a spell"—and threatens to have the same disastrous effect on the entire group, ringing through the minds "even of us who heard the words addressed to another." Their collective weakness in fending off the sexual advances of such a temptress leaves the men vulnerable—ready to sacrifice their reason, their control, and even their lives. Given the possibility of such losses, which would overturn the world that these men dominate, it is little wonder that they choose to solve the problem by destroying its source—the monstrously oversexed woman.

5.   Thus are we ministers of God's own wish: that the
     world, and men for whom His Son die, will not be
     given over to monsters, whose very existence would
     defame Him. He has allowed us to redeem one soul
     already, and we go out as the old knights of the Cross
     to redeem more. Like them we shall travel toward
     sunrise; and like them, if we fall, we fall in good cause.

Here, in Chapter XXIV, Van Helsing summarizes the nature of their
quest to Mina as they chase Dracula across Europe. To modern
readers, the professor's words sound like an exercise in hyperbole,
as he draws very bold lines between good and evil. However, Stoker
does, in fact, intend Dracula to be as much a cautionary moral tale
as a novel of horror and suspense. Deeply informed by the anxieties
of the Victorian age—the threat that scientific advancement posed
to centuries of religious tradition, and the threat that broadening
liberties for women posed to patriarchal society—Dracula makes
bold distinctions between the socially acceptable and the socially
unacceptable; between right and wrong; between holy and unholy.
Here, as Van Helsing likens his mission to one of "the old knights of
the Cross," we should understand him not as a bombastic windbag,
but as a product of genuine Victorian fear and righteousness.

QUOTATIONS

KEY FACTS

FULL TITLE
  Dracula

AUTHOR
  Bram Stoker

TYPE OF WORK
  Novel

GENRE
  Gothic, horror

LANGUAGE
  English

TIME AND PLACE WRITTEN
  1891–1897; London, England

DATE OF FIRST PUBLICATION
  1897

PUBLISHER
  Constable

NARRATOR
  Dracula is told primarily through a collection of journal entries, letters, and telegrams written or recorded by its main characters: Jonathan Harker, Mina Murray, Dr. John Seward, Lucy Westenra, and Dr. Van Helsing.

POINT OF VIEW
  Shifts among the first-person perspectives of several characters

TONE
  Gothic, dark, melodramatic, righteous

TENSE
  Though some of the entries record the thoughts and observations of the characters in the present tense, most incidents in the novel are recounted in the past tense.

SETTING (TIME)
  End of the nineteenth century

SETTING (PLACE)

England and Eastern Europe

PROTAGONIST

The members of Van Helsing's gang—Van Helsing, Jonathan Harker, John Seward, Arthur Holmwood, Mina Murray, and Quincey Morris —might be considered the novel's collective protagonist.

MAJOR CONFLICT

A vampire with diabolical ambitions preys upon a group of English and American do-gooders, threatening the foundations of their society until they dedicate themselves to ridding the Earth of his evil.

RISING ACTION

Jonathan Harker learns of Dracula's evil while visiting his castle to complete a real estate transaction; Lucy Westenra becomes increasingly ill under Dracula's spell

CLIMAX

Lucy is transformed into a vampire; Van Helsing and his comrades mercifully destroy her

FALLING ACTION

Van Helsing and company chase Dracula across Eastern Europe, where they eventually destroy him.

THEMES

The promise of Christian salvation; the consequences of modernity; the dangers of female sexual expression

MOTIFS

Blood; Christian iconography; science and superstition

SYMBOLS

The "weird sisters"; the stake driven through Lucy's heart; the Czarina Catherine

FORESHADOWING

The initially unidentifiable wounds on Lucy's neck fore-shadow her fall to the dark side by confirming Dracula's presence in England.

KEY FACTS

STUDY QUESTIONS & ESSAY TOPICS

STUDY QUESTIONS

1. *How does Count Dracula pervert elements of Christian tradition? What is the significance of this perversion?*

As a vampire, Dracula inverts one of the principal Catholic sacraments: holy Communion. Whereas Catholics believe that they are granted spiritual life by drinking the symbolic blood of Christ, Dracula prolongs and revitalizes his physical life by drinking the real blood of humans. While Christians consider flesh transient and secondary in importance to the eternal spirit, the soulless Dracula lives only for the flesh. The count's devotee, Renfield, dismisses the notion of a soul with a fervency that, we can only assume, he learned from his master. "To hell with you and your souls!" he shouts at Dr. Seward, "Haven't I got enough to worry, and pain, and distract me already, without thinking of souls?"

Renfield's inability to deal with "the consequence—the burden of a soul" is important because it helps frame Stoker's novel as a cautionary tale. Stoker lived in an age in which, due largely to advancements in science, people were equipped to question, if not dismiss outright, the religious doctrines that had formed the basis of moral and social order for centuries. In this sense, *Dracula* explores the anxieties of a society on the brink of moral collapse, suggesting that safety lies in the very religious traditions that modernity tempts society to abandon.

2.   *Discuss the role of sexuality in* Dracula. *What does the novel suggest about sexual behavior in Victorian England?*

Stoker explicitly links vampirism and sexuality from the early chapters of the novel, when the three vampire beauties visit Harker in Dracula's castle. Because the prejudices of his time barred him from writing frankly about intercourse, Stoker suggests graphic sexual acts through the predatory habits of his vampires. The means by which Dracula feeds, for instance, echo the mechanics of sex: he waits to be beckoned into his victim's bedroom, then he pierces her body in a way that makes her bleed. In the mind of the typical Victorian male, this act has the same effect as a real sexual encounter—it transforms the woman from a repository of purity and innocence into an uncontrollably lascivious creature who inspires "wicked, burning desire" in men. We witness such a transformation in Lucy Westenra, who becomes a dangerous figure of sexual predation bent on destroying men with her wanton lust. Because of her immoral mission, the men realize that Lucy must be destroyed.

In this sense, Stoker's novel betrays a deep-seated fear of women who go beyond the sexual boundaries Victorian society has proscribed for them. If women are not hopelessly innocent virgins, like Lucy before Dracula gets hold of her, or married, like Mina, they are whores who threaten to demolish men's reason and, by extension, their power. The fact that such temptresses are destroyed without exception in *Dracula* testifies to the level of anxiety Victorian men felt regarding women's sexuality.

QUESTIONS & ESSAYS

3. *Discuss Stoker's decision to recount the story of Dracula through journal entries, letters, and newspaper clippings. What are the strengths and drawbacks of this approach?*

The use of handwritten accounts of the principal characters, along with fictional newspaper clippings and telegrams, lends an air of authenticity to an otherwise fantastic story. Although this epistolary form makes the events of Dracula seem more real—or, in the very least, more intimate than they might have seemed if related by a single narrator—it does have several drawbacks. Though the different characters come from different social strata, and in some cases different countries, they nonetheless sound practically the same. The exceptions to this trend, such as Van Helsing and Morris, tend to speak with absurdly heavy and unbelievable accents. Although he proves less than talented in developing a symphony of strong, individual voices to relate his tale, Stoker manages to use the puzzlelike structure of the novel to create considerable suspense. We constantly wonder if the characters will piece together the mystery that we ourselves already understand.

Suggested Essay Topics

1. Discuss the appearances Dracula makes throughout the novel. What does Stoker achieve by keeping his title character in the shadows for so much of the novel?

2. Discuss Van Helsing's role as Dracula's antagonist. Why is the old Dutch professor the most threatening adversary to the count?

3. Discuss the roles of Mina Harker and Lucy Westenra. How are the women similar? How are they different? Why, in your opinion, is Lucy the first to fall under Dracula's spell?

4. Discuss *Dracula* in relation to modernity. What, for instance, are the novel's attitudes toward scientific advancements?

5. What is the role of geography in the novel? How do Stoker's choices of setting conform to the principles of Gothic fiction? How do they depart from these principles?

REVIEW & RESOURCES

QUIZ

1. At the inn in Bistritz, what does the innkeeper's wife give Harker to help him on his journey to Castle Dracula?

   A. A flask of Romanian wine
   B. A map of the region
   C. A bilingual dictionary
   D. A crucifix

2. Harker reports that the count's English estate is rather isolated, and neighbored only by what institution?

   A. A morgue
   B. An insane asylum
   C. A prison
   D. A brothel

3. Despite Dracula's warning, Harker falls asleep in a forbidden part of the castle. Who or what nearly attacks him there?

   A. Three voluptuous women
   B. An enormous bat
   C. A ferocious wolf
   D. An insane servant

4. How does Dracula react when Harker requests to leave the castle immediately?

   A. He refuses, telling Harker to prepare to die.
   B. He summons a seductive woman to distract Harker.
   C. He opens the door.
   D. He puts Harker into a deep trance.

5. Whom does Lucy Westenra agree to marry?

    A. Quincey Morris
    B. Arthur Holmwood
    C. John Seward
    D. Jonathan Harker

6. How does Dr. Seward diagnose his patient, Renfield?

    A. Zoöphagous maniac
    B. Schizophrenic
    C. Manic depressive
    D. Sociopath

7. How does the captain of the Demeter arrive in Whitby, England?

    A. He does not arrive in Whitby, but instead jumps into the sea during a terrifying storm.
    B. Insane, having been driven out of his mind by an "evildoer" who preyed on his crew
    C. Dead, with his hands tied to the wheel of the ship
    D. Dead, with his neck broken and a look of horror on his face

8. What does Mina assume has caused the two small wounds on Lucy's neck?

    A. An insect
    B. A shawl pin
    C. Human teeth
    D. A vampire bat

9. Where does Dr. Seward's patient, Renfield, go when he attempts to escape?

    A. To the chapel of the Carfax estate
    B. To a ruined bridge spanning the Thames
    C. To a graveyard on the outskirts of the city
    D. To Lucy Westenra's home

10. Who provides blood for Lucy Westenra's first transfusion?

    A. Lucy's mother
    B. Van Helsing
    C. John Seward
    D. Arthur Holmwood

11. How does Lucy Westenra's mother die?

    A. Lucy, transformed into a vampire, sucks her blood.
    B. She suffers a heart attack after a wolf appears in her daughter's bedroom window.
    C. She is swept out to sea by a sudden and terrible storm.
    D. She falls victim to Dr. Seward's patient, Renfield, who goes on a killing spree across the English countryside.

12. How does Van Helsing react when the dying Lucy asks Holmwood for a final kiss?

    A. He breaks down in tears and curses Lucy's sad fate.
    B. He insists that Arthur wear a garlic wreath before approaching Lucy.
    C. He pulls Holmwood away from Lucy, telling the young man to kiss her only on the forehead.
    D. He forbids Holmwood from kissing her, claiming that no one should disturb her beauty.

13. What name is given to the mysterious woman suspected of abducting children from Hampstead Heath?

    A. The Bloofer Lady
    B. The Hampstead Horror
    C. Witchie
    D. Queen Mab

14. What does Mina give Van Helsing to aid his investigation into the strange circumstances surrounding Lucy's death?

    A. A silver crucifix
    B. A large check
    C. Her husband's journals
    D. Her complete correspondence with Lucy

15. How does Van Helsing prove to Dr. Seward that Lucy Westenra is one of the "Un-Dead"?

    A. He holds a mirror up to her face to prove that she does not cast a reflection.

    B. He takes the young doctor to the cemetery to witness Lucy's predacious nighttime habits.

    C. He allows himself to be bitten by Lucy.

    D. He throws Lucy's body in the river, stating that the bodies of the "Un-Dead" sink like stones.

16. What happens to Lucy's body after Arthur Holmwood drives a stake through her heart?

    A. It turns to dust.

    B. It returns to its former beauty.

    C. It vanishes.

    D. It morphs into a bat and flies away.

17. After reading the Harkers' journals, whom does Dr. Seward suspect is under Dracula's spell?

    A. Renfield

    B. Van Helsing

    C. Jonathan Harker

    D. Arthur Holmwood

18. What role does Van Helsing first assign Mina in their quest to kill Dracula?

    A. She must seduce the count by leaving her bedroom window open at night.

    B. She must serve as the group's secretary and take dutiful notes.

    C. She must not be burdened or endangered by their quest and should take no part in it.

    D. She should go to the British Museum and find out all she can about the nosferatu.

19. What do Van Helsing and his men find in the chapel at the Carfax estate?

    A. The bodies of several small children
    B. Dozens of boxes of earth that Dracula has shipped from Transylvania
    C. The wolf that has escaped from the Zoological Gardens
    D. A shrine to the count erected by the madman Renfield

20. Why does Renfield become agitated during his conversation with Seward the night before he is attacked?

    A. Seward refuses to provide him with the sugar he needs to continue trapping flies.
    B. Seward asks him to account for the souls of the lives he plans to collect.
    C. He senses that Dracula is near and that he is in grave danger.
    D. He has received a letter from his wife and wishes to return to her immediately.

21. What do Van Helsing and company find when they break into the Harkers' bedroom in search of Dracula?

    A. A large bat fluttering about the room
    B. Mina and Jonathan in a deep sleep, their bodies covered by a thick, hazy mist
    C. Mina feeding from a cut on Dracula's chest
    D. Dracula drinking from Mina's neck

22. What is responsible for the scar on Mina's forehead?

    A. A Communion wafer
    B. A crucifix
    C. Dracula's teeth
    D. Count Voldemort's curse

23. How does Van Helsing's crew determine that Dracula has left England by ship?

   A. They bribe a porter at the docks, who reveals the count's whereabouts.
   B. In Piccadilly, they stumble upon the count's journal.
   C. Harker follows Dracula to the docks and watches him board a ship.
   D. Van Helsing hypnotizes Mina.

24. Who transports the count's body from Galatz toward Castle Dracula?

   A. A businessman named Immanuel Hildesheim
   B. A band of Gypsies
   C. The captain of the Czarina Catherine
   D. Transylvanian peasants

25. What do Mina and Jonathan Harker name their child?

   A. Junior
   B. Quincey
   C. Van
   D. Adam

REVIEW & RESOURCES

Suggestions for Further Reading

CARTER, MARGARET L. DRACULA: *The Vampire and the Critics.* Ann Arbor, Michigan: UMI Research Press, 1988.

LEATHERDALE, CLIVE. DRACULA: *The Novel and the Legend.* Wellingborough, Northamptonshire: Aquarian Press, 1985.

PUNTER, DAVID. *The Literature of Terror: A History of Gothic Fictions from 1765 to the Present Day.* London: Longman, 1980.

TWITCHELL, JAMES B. *The Living Dead: The Vampire in Romantic Literature.* Durham, North Carolina: Duke University Press, 1981.

SparkNotes Study Guides: